CHRISTINA'S COOKBOOK

CHRISTINA'S COOKBOOK
RECIPES *and* STORIES *from a* NORTHWEST ISLAND KITCHEN

CHRISTINA ORCHID

Foreword by JOYCE GOLDSTEIN ■ *Photographs by* MICHAEL SKOTT

SASQUATCH BOOKS
SEATTLE

for Bruce

Printed in China
Published by Sasquatch Books
Distributed by Publishers Group West
12 11 10 09 08 07 06 05 04   6 5 4 3 2 1

Photography: Michael Skott
Historical photographs courtesy of Christina Orchid
Book Design: Kate Basart
Display type set in Cursive, text set in Minion
Frontispiece: *Christina and her cousin Johnny after fishing in Cow Creek in the
channeled scablands of eastern Washington, about 1954.*

Library of Congress Cataloging-in-Publication Data
Orchid, Christina.
Christina's cookbook : recipes and stories from a Northwest Island kitchen / by Christina Orchid.
p. cm.
Includes index.
ISBN 1-57061-403-2
1. Cookery, American—Pacific Northwest style. I. Title.
TX715.2.P32O73 2004
641.59795—dc22
2004049557

SASQUATCH BOOKS
119 South Main Street, Suite 400 / Seattle, WA 98104 / (206) 467-4300
www.sasquatchbooks.com / custserv@sasquatchbooks.com

Contents

Foreword

I MET CHRISTINA ORCHID ELEVEN YEARS AGO, AT A FOOD CONFERENCE IN Istanbul organized by Oldways Preservation and Exchange Trust. Most of the attendees were food writers, nutritionists, academicians, and food purveyors. Christina and I bonded immediately as we were among the few working chefs in attendance. Because this was a time when women chefs were a bit of a rarity, we found that we had much in common: our passion for food, our use of fresh, seasonal ingredients, our support for local purveyors, our belief in simplicity of presentation, and our love of classic recipes. We also shared a particular wry sense of humor and a distaste for pretension and pomposity. We became friends and colleagues. AFTER THE CONFERENCE we joined a small group and traveled along the Mediterranean coast of Turkey, exploring ruins, poking around markets, shopping for rugs and crafts—and eating, of course. Christina and I ate and talked, ate and talked, ate and talked. We were not only working chefs, but also owners of our own establishments, with all of the financial and managerial responsibilities. This was a working vacation. We talked about menu planning, creating recipes, training staff, pleasing customers, and what we might bring back from this very enlightening trip. ALTHOUGH OUR INTERESTS AND GOALS were similar, the reality of our situations was quite different. Christina was running a very small place in an out-of-the-way spot in the Pacific Northwest. Her restaurant space was over a refurbished gas station on Orcas Island, in the San Juans and well to the north of Seattle. I was running a very big restaurant in the heart of downtown San Francisco, specializing in Mediterranean food at a time when most people didn't even know what countries were on the Mediterranean. Let us say that we both had challenges! We needed to educate our diners, but not in an academic or didactic way. We needed to seduce them with great

Christina Orchid, the day before Christina's opened, 1980.

food and fine service and hope that they would become regular clientele, a part of our extended family. **12:30** BESIDES LOCATING FIRST-RATE INGREDIENTS and maintaining our physical plant, we also needed to find a staff to share our beliefs and our passion. We needed to teach them to cook and to understand the food as we conceived it. As my Square One Restaurant was open for lunch and dinner, I was there every day for fourteen to fifteen hours. I, however, was not on the line. Want to talk about a labor of love? Christina Orchid has worked the line for twenty-five years. It's hard enough to open a restaurant in an obscure place and hope to have enough diners to stay in business. But to be in the kitchen and on the line—with just one other cook, every night for a quarter of a century—deserves applause, admiration, awe. The proof of her success and talent is that she is still there, cooking her heart out. Her feet may be a bit more tender, but her palate is clear and strong. **CHRISTINA HAS TRAVELED WIDELY** and has kept her eyes and her mouth open in France, Italy, Turkey, Russia, and elsewhere. Her culinary experience is considerable. But when I read the recipes in this fine personal book I keep hearing the refrain of "There's no place like home." And home is Orcas Island and the Pacific Northwest. Everything Christina cooks comes from nearby. She's had to build a network of suppliers. She knows every purveyor, every grower—and in a way they have become an integral part of Christina's restaurant. **CHRISTINA'S RECIPES ARE NOT REVOLUTIONARY.** There's no foam, no gel, no weird combinations. Her personal touches and interpretations of the classics are not egotistical displays but evidence of a fine sensibility about food. She knows how to get the most flavor from a dish, and when to stop. The recipes are not overly complicated and labor intensive. Remember, there are only two on the line in her professional kitchen, so you know they are not doing things the long way around just to make an impression. Christina's recipes deliver big flavor with not too much hard work. Since I cannot dine regularly at Christina's, I look forward to cooking many of her signature recipes. I know you will too.

—*Joyce Goldstein*

Acknowledgments

NO CHEF IS AN ISLAND, AND ONE DOES NOT RUN A RESTAURANT FOR so many years without lots of help in many shapes and forms. First I think of my partner in all things, Bruce, who gave up his job in politics to share in the life of the restaurant. His work and devotion have truly made the restaurant "ours." I will always be thankful for my parents, Payton and Emily Reid, who taught me the world really was my oyster. To the refrigeration specialists, plumbers, and electricians who came when we needed you; early, late, and in middle of service, you were there! Thank you! Brent Barry, who first showed me how to

Celebrating the 10th year of Christina's—staff past and present, 1990.

fillet salmon "Indian style," and Drewie, who has minced crab and spot prawns for years, deserve special thanks. To the farmers, who have toiled long and hard to give us the wonder of produce absolutely unavailable in the markets, we owe much: Horse Drawn, Morningstar, Rainwater Farms, Orcas Farm, Marion Wiseman for Haricot and Broadbeans, thank you. To our friends who bucked us up even when they didn't know we needed it: Fred, Betsy and Nancy, David and Catherine, Wally and Susan, Dickie and L. S. D., Gretchen K., Polly, Freddie and Amelia, Charles and Laurana, and Michael De we send love. A special note to my son, Peter, who endured years of dishwashing and did homework by dim light in the back room, and still chose the life of an artist. Special kudos to Tony Davis for his counsel and support during the process. At Sasquatch, I have Suzanne de Galan to thank for convincing me I had something to add to the already bulging bookshelf, Gary Luke for spurring me on, and Terence Maikels for his guidance. I thank Michael Skott for his fine photographs. The Christina's staff, past and present, from whom I learned so much: Jennifer, Lois, Joy, Tom, Libby, Jean Louis and Corinne, Jay, Kelly, Christopher, Gregory, Lucy and Mary, Ross, Steve, Ratso, Jacob and Christi, John and Mr. Clean, and especially Ty and Andrew who kept it going while I worked on this book. Most of all, my heartfelt thanks to the wonderful folks who have found their way up the stairs, spread the word, and kept coming back. They made the restaurant and my life as a chef glorious and rewarding.

Introduction

I GREW UP IN THE PACIFIC NORTHWEST CORNER OF THE UNITED States in the middle of the twentieth century, a golden age, to be sure. My parents, barely removed from the farm, brought their frugal country values to our suburban house. My mother prepared nutritious and conscientious meals three times a day. My father was home for dinner every day at the same time. While my brothers played, I was expected to help my mother "in the kitchen." Her diligence in the backyard garden produced countless meals, mostly forgotten, save for the tomatoes, warm and dripping, which still run down my chin, forty years later. EACH SUMMER WE MADE THE TRIP from Portland up the Columbia Gorge past Celilo Falls to the Wallula Gap where the Snake and the Columbia Rivers merge and cut through the scablands of eastern Washington to my grandparents ranch on the Benge-Hooper Road. It was a long, hot drive, but by the time we clunked over the cattle crossing under the branded wooden gate and followed the lane down through the shade of the Lombardy poplars to the big house, the late afternoon cooled and we could hear the race of Cow Creek and the bang of the screen door as my grandmother came to greet us. It was an idyll. Of course we never knew it. In between moving irrigation pipe and working cattle I spent my time in the cookhouse. There, three meals a day were prepared for the ranch hands, cowboys, family members, visiting dignitaries, and

My grandfather, Ralph Snyder, after a successful bird hunt, about 1915, Spokane, Washington.

anybody else around at mealtimes. The best cowboys and hands wanted to work where the food was good. It was never any big deal that all the eggs and milk, cream, cottage cheese and butter, beef, chicken, pork, sausage and bacon, vegetables, all came from right there on the ranch. That was the only way to run a good outfit and make it profitable. Making butter just meant sitting on the screen porch for an hour cranking the churn till your arm burned, straining to hear your favorites through the static on the little radio tuned to a Spokane station over a hundred miles away. IT WAS DURING THIS TIME that I yearned to live in a penthouse in New York, dine at the Sherry Netherland, shop at Bendel's, take taxis, and live the life of my destiny, which I had created from reading *The New York Times Sunday* edition, *The New Yorker*, and *Eloise*. I had no idea there were girls just my age living in New York City, dreaming of living on a ranch and working cattle on horseback. Dining in a restaurant was an extremely rare event during my childhood. So, naturally, I loved restaurants. Thrilled to be choosing from a giant menu, I carefully minded my manners and took stock of the decor, the waiters, and the other diners. My father always pointed out things like a refilled ketchup bottle or a dirty fork and silently fumed over sloppy service. ▨ WHEN MY PARENTS BOUGHT A FARM in Westsound on Orcas Island on the opposite side of the state, it was the end of our Portland summers. While my father toiled in the city, my brothers and I were either at the ranch or on the island. On the island we water skied and got into trouble by driving around and drinking beer—the time-honored rite of passage for youth. On the ranch we sweated and scratched at the cheatgrass, moved irrigation pipe, baled hay, and moved cattle on horseback. For recreation we took our inner tubes down Cow Creek and experimented with explosives. ▨ MY GRANDMOTHER ADVISED against homemaking and typing classes in school. She said if I knew how to type, I would just end up being a secretary, and homemaking was learned at home. I went to art school, because I loved to paint and make pottery. Later, when I was still young and divorced, with a toddler in tow, I wished for some skills that would make me employable. When I started cooking, I was inspired by the stories of the great chefs. I wanted to go and apprentice but I couldn't find a babysitter. Instead I was a reader. I read all the great chefs and from their stories gained inspiration and insight into the lives of restaurateurs and chefs. It was a life that appealed to me: finding and preparing the foods of my region (Fernand Point, Paul Prudhomme) in simple and flavorful ways (M. F. K. Fischer, Richard Olney), in a dining room without pretense or snobbery (Ludwig Bemelmans, Gael Greene), in a conscientious, forthright way (Henri-Paul Pellaprat, Seymour Britchsky), allowing the flavor of the ingredients themselves to shine (Elizabeth David, Colman Andrews), and providing service conducive to anticipation, relaxation, and pleasure (A. J. Liebling, Angelo Pellegrini, Quentin Crewe), all in an atmosphere of welcome, warmth, and sharing (George Lang, Calvin Trillin). ▨ MAKING CHOICES IS AN IMPORTANT PART OF A LIFE. Luckily for me, I was forced to make choices, which is sometimes the easiest way, though some may not think so. I always worked in restaurants. Well, restaurants is kind of a high-falutin word for some of the places I worked. I was fired from a Tastee Freeze for making the soft ice cream cones too big. In my first cooking job, I would regularly make, fire, and plate a hundred and thirty Reuben sandwiches in an hour or so. And talk to customers lined up at the bar while I did. ▨ I WAITED TABLES at the Tok Junction in Alaska, where serving the wrong bourbon could put you up against the wall with a gun at your temple. I did time in a gentle corporate park where we operated twenty-six cafeterias and most of my days were spent checking steam tables with a thermometer and packing and unpacking frozen aluminum trays full of veal cutlets, chicken-fried steaks, and hamburgers, all of which looked remarkably alike. ▨ IN DECEMBER OF 1979 I leased a three-bedroom apartment on the waterfront in the small village of Eastsound on Orcas Island in the far northwest corner of Washington State with the intention of turning it into a crêperie cum coffeehouse. The apartment was one of six spaces deemed commercial waterfront. The other five were already occupied. I was shaky and fairly impoverished, just coming off a hurtful divorce. A newspaper article encouraged me to assess my real talents before beginning a new venture. I came up with two. I had real good taste and I could cook. Also, I had worked in restaurants my entire adult life. I was thirty-three years old, the single mother of an eighth grader. I had been living on the island for four years. I hired a carpenter and went to work. In Washington State we have the Shoreline Management Act, which requires a lengthy permit process before any construction

Cousin Willy, Brother Billy, and me, Thanksgiving hunt, Bar U Ranch, 1956.

Cooking brunch at Christina's, 1983.

takes place near the shore. I was plenty daunted by the work of opening a restaurant and had neither time nor money to do any major remodeling. Instead our changes were cosmetic. We pulled off the woodwork and planed it to remove the paint. I scraped the linoleum off the floors; clear, vertical-grain fir lay underneath, cheap flooring when the place was built as a combination machine shop, filling station, and boat ways in the early 1930s. We changed a doorway so it led into one of the front bedrooms instead of the living room. The bedroom became an entry and we removed the closet that separated that room from the bedroom next to it; that room became the bar. The linen closet became the waiter's station, the built-in desk became the booth at table 4, the laundry room turned easily into a dish pit, and the bathroom became . . . well, the bathroom. My friend Jennifer covered some plywood panels with fabric and upholstered around the bathtub, which I promptly filled with plants. We worked on the restaurant all that spring without making one structural change. I haunted the restaurant supply places in Seattle with my trusty measuring tape, trying to find equipment that would fit the twelve-by-ten kitchen. THAT SPRING, as the rooms of the restaurant began to take shape, so did my ideas about the restaurant. I didn't want to make crepes; I wanted to make real food. I wanted to take what I loved about the island and show all that were interested that the food I grew up with in the "out West" of America could be every bit as wonderful as the places in France and New York that were regarded with such awe—fresh sockeye, local oysters, clams from the island—instead of the breaded, frozen, and deep-fried lumps that were sold everywhere as the "Captain's Platter." Ripe tomatoes, real whipped cream, good beefsteak, potatoes that tasted like the ones from the garden, and real chives, not green onions, and plates where the beauty of the food was the garnish and with no sauces covering up everything. In fact, maybe no sauces at all; just good salt and fresh herbs. The service would be good, people would feel taken care of so they could relax. We would create an oasis of the genuine in a world fraught with jive. I had no idea what I was getting into, even though I thought I did. IT HAS BEEN ALMOST TWENTY-FIVE YEARS since I opened the doors to Christina's, and today the restaurant is still very much as it was then. Oh the menu is constantly changing, we have a new kitchen and a fabulous collection of copper, the chairs are more comfortable and we have more of them. The glassware is better and the plates are bigger. The food world has shifted on its axis and I can buy ingredients from all over the world just by picking up the phone or going online—even though I still prefer to use what I get from right here on the island. But still no yacht harbor or condominiums out the windows, just a few more lights twinkle at night. The view hasn't changed at all, although with the weather and the seasons it never looks the same way twice. We have more customers, but they are still the adventurous ones, willing to climb the stairs over the gas station in the island village of Eastsound. And still, as I remind my staff every day, we are only as good as the last plate that goes out of the kitchen.

IN THE KITCHEN, WE KEEP A BULLETIN BOARD WITH AN OPEN envelope tacked to it. Into this envelope go the names and addresses of all the people who want copies of recipes. Every so often I actually get it together and write one down for someone. This happens when they make a lot of noise or are from some big publication that I feel will provide good exposure for the restaurant. It is always a hassle because most of my days are spent in the kitchen in front of the stove. The closest computer is on my desk at home, miles away. IT HAS BEEN SEVERAL YEARS since I was first asked to produce a cookbook. In preparing this book, the first thing I did was remember all the earnest eaters who requested recipes. My apologies go out to all of them for the time it took to put it together. In twenty years, the stack of requests has grown into a box and most of those requests remain unanswered. The box was the beginning of this book. Inside were thousands of recipe requests and bundles of recipes. Written on the backs of old menus, stained and torn pieces of notebook paper with no name or instructions, just a list of ingredients, usually in large amounts or often with no amounts, just proportions. These were notes written for the staff or for myself to remember, things like: "It was the cloves that gave the poached fish that certain je ne sais quoi." Beside the realization that the same recipes were requested again and again (the Chocolate Blackout Torte on page 230), there were dishes I hadn't made in years or things I had only made once or twice. There were appetizers that were on the menu for years, because folks would whine when we took them off, that are now so dated and yet so good they are almost ready to be reborn as the latest "hot" trend (Picnic Terrine could be one). There are soups I made a thousand times and never made the same way twice.

I REALIZE NOW I have my pet foods and ingredients, tried and true herbs and cooking methods. For me this book became a kind of journey. In preparing the recipes I took a trip through my past and began to understand how my experiences in the world had formed my attitudes about cooking and eating. Chefs are always asked how they came up with the ideas for dishes. I was astonished to discover that an overheard comment, or the memory of a platter of fried fish, or a piece of bread stuffed with lamb eaten on the beach in Greece could have provided me with a flavor memory and inspiration, sometimes years later! The foundation, backbone, and background of my tastes had been fostered by my family; it was purely accidental that the same values espoused by my parents and grandparents in regard to food and dining and community would be exactly what I needed to be a successful chef and business person. And my friends, like "the last of the millionaire playboys," who, among other things, introduced me to the pleasures of the table at a time in my life when I was dining on cold cereal three times a day. Or my friend I refer to in the book as "the tomato mogul," producer of mega-blockbusters, as genuine and down to earth as they come, gardener extraordinaire, who changed everybody's awareness of the plight of killer whales kept in captivity and found time to make soup for me when I needed it. The great good people in my dining room educated me beyond what is believable. I learned to listen carefully to comments about the food. I always enjoyed hearing how great and fabulous it was but I was also listening for comments about the texture or the juxtaposition of flavors. This is what has made me better as a chef, and so it continues, each day I learn and I get better. After twenty-five years at the stoves, I realize I am still figuring things out, every day. It is the true and sparkling thing about cooking. It is always new; there is always more to try, to make, to do, to savor. █▓█ FOR THE MOST PART I have kept the recipes in the following pages simple. This is not a paean to the inexperienced cook but rather the outgrowth of my own kitchen experiences. Use the very best ingredients you can find. Mess with them little. Do what is necessary to give those foodstuffs honor. Show them the way to greatness lies in a little salt, a little oil, just enough heat or chilling, some fresh herbs for accent. Like all the arts, cooking with passion and desire will always make up for lack of knowledge or experience. There lies the real secret of the kitchen.

Me on "Brownie." Bar U Ranch, about 1960. Though I didn't know how to use the rope, it was always on the saddle.

Christina's Pantry

House Ketchup
Herbes de Provence
Bar U Ranch Mustard
Homemade Mayonnaise
Piccalilli Relish
Cipolline Onion Relish
Chipotle Cocktail Sauce
Pickled Ginger
Blueberry Chutney
Fennel Breadsticks
Olive Flatbread
Hungarian Butterhorns
Shortbread
Chocolate Sauce
Raspberry Sauce

House Ketchup

In 1983 or so, I was thrilled when I bought our first island lamb from Coffelt Farm. I was really excited when Syd Coffelt also handed me a tub of lamb kidneys soaking in water. I raced back to my kitchen and immediately pulled down the old tomes to see what they had to say about *rognons* (lamb kidneys).

The next day I went in early to start the sauce. I had consulted the masters, and I knew what to do. The *rognons* would be fabulous. By the time I chalked "grilled *rognons*" on our board that night, I was one with my little kitchen universe. Sure enough, the first ticket into the kitchen was for two *rognons* and two salmon. It was only a little while after the plates went out that Lois, the waiter, appeared in the kitchen and somewhat sheepishly asked if we had a bottle of ketchup.

My shoulders were sagging as I rummaged in the back of the refrigerator for the ketchup. After I handed it over, I took a peek through the curtain at table 9, where my precious *rognons* were being drenched with a bottled sauce. Two big, happy-looking guys in John Deere hats and overalls were having a laugh with their wives. They were dining with joy and gusto, exactly what I wanted in my dining room. I decided I would investigate making ketchup. Nowadays the staff seems to use most of it.

> *2 cans (16 ounces each) tomato paste*
> *2 cups water*
> *1¾ cups aged red wine vinegar*
> *½ cup balsamic vinegar*
> *1 tablespoon dry mustard*
> *1 teaspoon ground cinnamon*
> *1 teaspoon ground cumin*
> *⅛ teaspoon ground cloves*
> *⅛ teaspoon ground mace*
> *1¾ cups brown sugar*

IN A LARGE POT, combine the tomato paste, water, red wine and balsamic vinegars, mustard, cinnamon, cumin, cloves, and mace. Whisk well and add the brown sugar. Cook over medium heat for 20 minutes or so, until the flavors marry. Remove from the heat and cool for 10 minutes, then pour into glass bottles with tight-fitting lids. Store in sealed containers in the refrigerator.

Note: The ketchup can also be canned using standard canning procedures.

Makes about 6 cups

Pantries

AS A CHILD, I WAS OFTEN SENT TO THE PANTRY FOR A JAR OF TOMATOES, down the stairs, across the cold breezeway, and into the dark room where the hum of the freezer was company. I needed to use a stepstool to climb onto the freezer to get to the cupboard. On the bottom shelves were cans from the grocery store that were easily recognizable—tuna, olives, sardines. But the other shelves, the ones that went all the way to the ceiling, were packed solid with canning jars, mostly big, mostly without labels. I recognized the tomatoes, giant red orbs pressed to the glass in pale pink liquid. I would carry them carefully to my mother, for spaghetti sauce. MY GRANDMOTHER'S PANTRY WAS A MAGICAL PLACE. Hams hung from the ceiling. Everything from bear lard to foie gras rested on the shelves. The freezer was a vault, containing all the cuts of beef you could imagine, and some you couldn't, and fish from expeditions dating back to the fifties. My grandparents saved their ranch in the thirties by making sausage instead of selling the hogs on the hoof, so there was plenty of sausage, and bacon from the smokehouse up on the hill too. MY MOTHER, MY AUNTS, AND MY GRANDMOTHER were all veteran canners. Today, at eighty-four, my mother is still drying plums and making chili sauce. If you visit my Aunt GG, she will make you a breakfast of elk sausage, fiery with peppers, eggs from her chickens, and homemade biscuits with wild plum jam. She is eighty-three and her husband is ninety-one. They've quit growing anything but corn, tomatoes, and cucumbers in their garden; everything else was "too much work," they said. They have a pantry in their double-wide, and when you leave you'll be carrying jars of watermelon pickles, pickled steelhead, chow-chow, the aforementioned elk sausage, and anything else you may have professed a vague interest in. My aunt Stevie,

My grandmother, Aimee Snyder, feeding puppy and pig at the Hilltop Wheat Ranch, about 1918.

who still lives on the Bar U Ranch, makes tacos from grass-fed beef and harvests her own asparagus from a plot that is forty years old. Her garden is the size of a city lot, and the basement pantry shelves are full from floor to ceiling. The cowboys and harvest crews may be long gone, but a way of life remains.

Herbes de Provence

If I were marooned on a desert island with just ten ingredients, I would make sure this herb mixture was one of them. Herbes de Provence are just that, the herbs of Provence, the fabled hillside region in the south of France where the herbs struggle for water and nutrients in the rocky soil, and relentless sunshine gives the leaves a density of flavor impossible to reproduce in our well-watered, composted gardens. It's not enough that France has given us the repertoire of great sauces and the elegant, refined touchstones of grand cuisine, we also get the robust and vital flavors of the earth as well. This herb mixture is great sprinkled on things you are going to roast or grill—lamb, chicken, fish, even toast!

> *½ cup thyme*
> *1½ cups dried lavender flowers*
> *½ cup dried sage leaves, crumbled*
> *1½ cups whole fennel seed*
> *¾ cup whole dried rosemary*
> *1½ cups dried oregano leaves*
> *¼ cup whole marjoram*

TOSS THE HERBS TOGETHER in a bowl and store in a container with a tight-fitting lid. The herbs will lose their intensity of flavor over time. Use them within 6 months or discard them.

Makes about 6½ cups

Bar U Ranch Mustard

Family legend has it that this mustard and a kind of white fudge called divinity were the two food items my grandmother knew how to prepare when she arrived at the ranch as a young bride in 1918. Once I asked her how she ever figured out how to cook for a harvest crew, and she said she followed recipes and that she threw a lot of stuff in the pigs' bucket. By the time I was old enough to pay attention, my grandmother was an accomplished cook who loved Julia Child and read *Larousse Gastronomique* because it was interesting. This is her mustard. Deceptively simple, it must sit for at least a month for the vinegar to "cook" the flour and for the mustard flavor to mellow.

2 cups unbleached white flour
2 cups cider vinegar
2 cups firmly packed brown sugar
2 cups dry mustard

IN A LARGE BOWL, combine the flour, vinegar, brown sugar, and dry mustard and whisk together until there are no lumps and the mixture is completely smooth. Because of the amount of vinegar used, canning is not necessary. Put the mustard in pint jars with tight-fitting lids. Let it cure at room temperature for at least 1 month before using. If there is any separation, simply remix it. The flavor improves with age.

Makes 2 pints

Homemade Mayonnaise

Well, why not make your own mayonnaise? Although Julia Child is quoted as saying that making mayonnaise is so easy a stunned monkey could do it, that is not exactly true.

As with so many exquisitely simple things, there is much at stake here: the quality, size, and freshness of the eggs; the type of mustard; the delicate question of sugar and the "just right" amount of salt; and the quality, type, and flavor of the oil. These factors don't even take into account the barometer, which, rising or falling, can affect the emulsification process in such a subtle way that you are never sure whether it's the weather or your lack of skill that's to blame when it doesn't work.

You can make mayonnaise in a bowl with a whisk, but I never would: I am way too lazy and I simply don't have the time. The food processor has changed the way we cook and eat, and among the chores it does so beautifully is making mayonnaise.

If you get into the habit of making your own mayonnaise, you will customize the recipe to suit yourself.

4 large egg yolks
2 teaspoons salt
3 tablespoons fresh lemon juice
2 tablespoons Dijon mustard
2 cups peanut oil or other oil with a neutral flavor

IN A FOOD PROCESSOR OR BLENDER, purée the eggs with the salt and lemon juice on high for 2 minutes, until completely smooth, then add the mustard. If the egg mixture gets warm from the action of the blade, stop and chill the mixture before continuing. With the motor running, pour in the oil in a slow, steady stream. The mixture should thicken at just about the time the oil runs out. Refrigerated, the mayonnaise will keep for at least a week.

Makes about 2 cups

Variation

For lemon mayonnaise, add the grated zest of 2 lemons.

The Vinegar Keg

I SPENT AN HOUR THE OTHER EVENING GETTING THE VINEGAR OUT OF my wooden keg. Every chef knows that vinegar is *the secret ingredient*. The four flavors we humans can really taste are sweet, sour, salty, and bitter. Everything else is smell. So I had the brilliant idea several years ago of making my own vinegar. I would do this by pouring dribs and drabs of leftover wine into this beautiful little wooden keg that came to the restaurant full of Beaujolais from Joseph Drouhin. The wine disappeared within a week, so I brought the keg home. After all, was this not why I had finally remodeled our kitchen? My wonderful pantry with oodles of counter space was perfect for fulfilling my vision of resourceful country living. The little keg sat there in all its glory. ⬛ NOW, YOU NEED TO KNOW THAT restaurateurs and chefs are given samples of wine by distributors who want us to buy these wines and put them on our wine list. With the recent explosion in the wine industry—due, in fact, to well-fed and well-invested boomers yearning to be winemakers, or, better yet, vineyard owners—there is a definite glut of wine on the market, much of it with bad labels and cutesy names. Winemakers need to know that no matter how great their wine is it is never going to sell if the label looks like NASCAR and the title of their efforts sounds like something from Nora Roberts. Of course, in that regard, I am usually all wrong; these are probably going to be hallmarks of next year's "hottest" wines. Well, leave me out. I don't like "hot" wine. However, my husband, *El Permanente,* and I, out of a willingness to support and encourage other creative souls, will taste anything and everything. In short, this means we have a never-ending supply of wine that we may or may not drink. I filled my little keg in short order and added half a glass of my favorite sherry vinegar from Spain, Jimenez. 🕙 MY LITTLE KEG SOON STARTED PRODUCING. Making salad dressing, I would simply walk to the pantry and smugly fill my cruet with my special vinegar. All was well for a year or so. Then, one evening, racing to finish the *beurre rouge* before the magazine people arrived, I turned the spigot and— nothing! I gently shook the keg. It was seriously full, heavy with liquid. I sloshed it. Nothing worked. The spigot, open full bore, was dry. Luckily, I found some cider vinegar in the cleaning bin and made do. 🕙 IT WASN'T UNTIL I PICKED UP A BOTTLE OF MERLOT the next day, still a third full, that I remembered the problem with my keg. I took the wine to the pantry and removed the cork from the top of the keg. The aroma floated out and filled the room. I peered inside. Total blackness. The spigot was still open and there was a minuscule droplet dried on the countertop. It took a phone call to winemaker and yeast sciences expert Kay Simon and a dip into *Larousse Gastronomique,* the last word on all things culinary, to clear up my little mystery: A harmless, sticky, bacterial mat known as the *maitre de vinaigre*—the "mother of vinegar"— had formed and was busily doing its job of turning wine into vinegar. Unfortunately, it had gotten out of control. It had literally devoured the vinegar and transformed it into something akin to the Blob. Figuring out how to deal with it was another matter. **11:31** *EL PERMANENTE HELD THE 6-LITER KEG UPSIDE DOWN* for almost an hour while I pulled and tugged at the gelatinous mass. Fortunately, I had a long pair of tweezers (ordered from the Williams-Sonoma catalog for just this sort of thing), which I used to pull the "mother" from the keg. After removing all of it, I strained and bottled the remaining vinegar and started over. **11:31** TODAY THE KEG AGAIN SITS PRISTINE, back in its place in the pantry, the remnants of last night's Château Faiveley safely in its belly.

The vinegar keg.

Piccalilli Relish

You can make this only in late summer when the garden has started to go and the afternoon light gets low and long. I like canning, pickling, and preserving. It's a ritual that satisfies some very basic need to get ready for winter. We use this relish in the restaurant as a component in various dishes, and it's good on burgers too.

2 quarts green tomatoes
⅔ cup salt
2 red bell peppers, seeded and cut into ⅛-inch dice
2 red onions, cut into ⅛-inch dice
1 tablespoon ground cloves
1 tablespoon ground cinnamon
1 tablespoon ground allspice
1 tablespoon freshly ground black pepper
1 tablespoon ground ginger
1 tablespoon dry mustard
2 cups firmly packed brown sugar
2 cups cider vinegar

CORE THE GREEN TOMATOES and chop them into fine dice, ¼ inch or smaller. Put them in a bowl, cover with the salt, and refrigerate overnight.

THE NEXT DAY, drain the tomatoes in a colander. In a large pot, combine the tomatoes, peppers, onions, cloves, cinnamon, allspice, pepper, ginger, and mustard. Mix well and add the brown sugar and vinegar.

BRING TO A BOIL and cook for 20 minutes or so, stirring occasionally. Preserve following standard canning procedures. May be refrigerated for up to 3 weeks.

Makes about 6 pints

Cipolline Onion Relish

Any onions can be used for this recipe as long as they are small. I like the cipolline because they are small and sweet and are grown in abundance at Morning Star Farm here on Orcas Island. Owners Steve and Mimi Diepenbrock have been supplying the restaurant for more than ten years now. That is a good long time for any small-scale farmer to keep it going. Over the years, we have watched as many idealistic young farmers have burned out, usually after just a season or so. Farming is easily as daunting as running a restaurant, with the same time crunch, long hours, hard physical labor, unforgiving profit margins, and highly perishable inventory. Fortunately for us, we have several farms here in the San Juans that provide us with a never-ending supply of good and beautiful produce. Nothing is so inspiring for a chef as cases of gorgeous green, purple, blue, yellow, and red fruits and vegetables heaped in all their simple glory on the back stairs just waiting for the gentle transformation into a magical meal.

2 pounds cipolline or pearl onions, blanched (see Chef's Tip) and peeled
½ cup red wine vinegar
½ cup red wine
1 cup firmly packed brown sugar
1 cinnamon stick, broken
6 cloves garlic, crushed but whole
1 cup golden raisins
1 bay leaf
8 whole cloves

PREHEAT THE OVEN TO 275°F. In a nonreactive roasting pan, combine all ingredients. Cover the pan tightly with foil and roast for 2 hours. Take the pan out of the oven, remove the foil, then return it to the oven for 10 minutes more, or until half the liquid evaporates. Store in a sealed container in the refrigerator, or can using standard canning procedures.

Makes about 6 cups

Chef's Tip: To blanch the onions drop them in boiling water and continue cooking until the water returns to a boil. Cook for one minute then drain and chill. Peel by cutting the root end of the onion off and slipping the peel down the sides. You should be left with the onion whole, the layers held together just above where the root was trimmed.

Chipotle Cocktail Sauce

This is a barn burner if you want it to be. As long as the flavor of the seafood is going to be buried, it might as well go down big and fiery. Just vary the amount of chipotle. I find that one is plenty for me, but then I don't like much heat. This sauce goes well with seafood you don't want to taste too much of, and big, blowsy drinks that leave you hooting and pink.

> *1 to 2 dried chipotle peppers (smoked jalapeño)*
> *⅓ cup water*
> *2 cups House Ketchup (see page 2)*
> *2 tablespoons prepared horseradish*
> *Juice and grated zest of 1 lemon*

IN A SMALL, nonreactive bowl, soak the chipotles in the water for 3 hours or overnight.

ADD THE WATER and chipotles to the ketchup and purée with an immersion blender or food processor. Heat gently in a small saucepan for 10 minutes, long enough for the flavors to marry. Chill.

FOLD IN THE HORSERADISH and lemon. The sauce will keep, stored in a sealed container in the refrigerator, for several weeks.

Makes 2 cups

Pickled Ginger

It is easy to buy pickled ginger, especially if you have access to an Asian grocery. We have several in Seattle, big, beautiful, modern stores full of wonderful things and usually the best selection of really fresh seafood in town. It is also simple to make your own pickled ginger, and it keeps, covered, in the refrigerator very well. It often imparts a more intense gingery flavor than the fresh stuff, and you get to choose when you buy and pickle the ginger, which allows you to buy the freshest and the best. Look for roots that are big and plump, with little scarring and no trace of wrinkles.

> *8 ounces fresh ginger*
> *3 cups water*
> *1½ cups rice wine vinegar*
> *4 cups sugar*

PEEL THE GINGER and slice it as thinly as possible, using a knife or mandoline. In a large pot, bring the water, vinegar, and sugar to a boil. Add the ginger slices and cook over medium heat for 10 minutes. Let cool, then store in the refrigerator. Pickled ginger will keep well in the refrigerator indefinitely if tightly sealed.

Makes about 4 cups

Blueberry Chutney

Chutney is a tasty thing to have up your culinary sleeve. Good on crackers or with grilled fish, it also can make a turkey sandwich something special. It can be served warm, cold, or at room temperature. It can be refrigerated, frozen, or preserved and given as a gift.

Blueberries are a Pacific Northwest icon. Their season is short, but when it comes around the harvest is rich and sweet. This chutney is a way to savor the dog days of summer all winter long.

½ cup red wine vinegar
1 cup honey
½ cup sugar
½ cup spicy white wine, such as Gewürztraminer or Riesling
2 cups chopped red onion
1 tablespoon minced garlic
1 small red chile, crushed, or dried crushed chiles to taste (about
    ½ teaspoon)
1 cinnamon stick
1 teaspoon peeled, grated ginger
1 tablespoon whole coriander seeds
5 pints blueberries
1 cup golden raisins

IN A LARGE, nonreactive pot, bring the vinegar, honey, sugar, wine, onion, garlic, chile, cinnamon stick, ginger, and coriander seeds to a boil. Reduce the heat and simmer for 30 minutes, until reduced slightly. Add the blueberries and raisins and cook gently for 10 minutes. Store in the refrigerator in a jar with a tight-fitting lid for up to 3 weeks, or can it in pint jars following standard canning procedures. The flavor improves with age.

Makes about 6 pints

Fennel Breadsticks

Having enough fresh bread every evening at Christina's has been my culinary *bête noir*. My dictum about having it in copious quantities, the never empty breadbasket, as part of the restaurant's identity, has sent me sobbing to the back stairs more than once. Bread that was never delivered, or burned. Getting fifty walk-ins on what we thought would be a slow winter night.

These breadsticks had their origin on one of those nights when we ran out of bread early in the evening. During a lull, I dumped some yeast and warm water into the food processor, added salt and some flour, and turned the thing on. As it processed, I poured in more water until a ball of dough formed. I let it go around a few minutes, pulled it out, flopped it on a floured counter, and sprinkled it with fennel seeds. I ran over to the hot line and turned the lamb chops on the grill, then hustled back to roll the dough out and cut it into thin strips. I laid the strips cut side up on an oiled sheet pan, shoved the pan in the oven, ran to the other side of the kitchen to pull four salmon fillets from the fire, plated them with their sauce and vegetables, then turned and removed the breadsticks from the oven. The breadsticks had puffed up and turned faintly golden at the edges. No kneading, no rising, nothing. They had a crumbly yet soft texture, kind of like pizza dough. They were light and incredibly tender. Better yet, the rolling and cutting eliminated the time-consuming task of forming the sticks. And they looked just fine.

After a little fine-tuning of the recipe, the fennel breadsticks became part of our breadbasket.

Chef's Tip: It's important not to knead the dough any longer than a minute or so. Unlike regular bread dough, with this one you do not want to develop the gluten.

> *1 tablespoon yeast*
> *1 tablespoon salt*

1 cup water
¼ cup good-quality olive oil
3 to 3½ cups unbleached white flour
1 tablespoon fennel seeds
1 tablespoon dried oregano

The bread basket.

IN A LARGE BOWL, mix the yeast, salt, water, and oil together and let sit for 5 minutes or so while the yeast and salt dissolve. Mix in the flour, then turn out onto a floured board and finish mixing by turning the dough with your hands. Knead in the fennel seeds and oregano. The dough should be rather sticky. Let rest for 5 minutes or so. At this point you can refrigerate the dough for up to 24 hours.

WHEN YOU'RE READY TO BAKE the breadsticks, preheat the oven to 400°F. Oil a sheet pan. On a floured surface, roll out the dough to a thickness of about ½ inch. Use a knife to cut the dough into slender sticks about ¼ inch wide. Place the pieces of dough on the sheet pan, cut sides up. Let the sticks rest at room temperature for 10 minutes or so, then bake for 7 to 10 minutes, until puffy and just barely colored at the edges. Serve hot.

Makes about 30 breadsticks

About Seasoning

SALT IS THE SINGLE MOST IMPORTANT SEASONING YOU CAN USE IN THE kitchen. There are lots of different kinds of salt available now. I prefer sea salt, which I have used forever at the restaurant. It is a clear briny salt with a hint of minerals, and a slight taste of stone (run your tongue along a dry smooth rock) that comes from being evaporated along rocky coastlines. Lots of young culinary school chefs like kosher salt, which I think they must use in the schools; it is way too salty for me. I think using the same salt all the time increases your familiarity with what it does and will give you the needed touch to "salt to taste." TAST-ING IS THE NEXT MOST IMPORTANT THING YOU CAN DO in the kitchen. Flavor is subjective and you should flavor food to suit yourself. Developing a palate is what cooking is really all about and this is done by tasting and tasting again. You will soon learn the flavors of various herbs and what they do when you add them to other flavors. Pepper is most often misused in the kitchen. It is especially true of inexperienced cooks who are far too generous with the pepper grinder in an effort to put some flavor on the plate. Big mistake. Fresh herbs of almost any kind will brighten food better than pepper. Oh, and that iodized table salt? Get rid of it!

Olive Flatbread

I am a big fan of flatbread, especially this one, which has become a regular part of our breadbasket. With the crackers (see page 34) and breadsticks (see page 19), it makes a trio of simple and rustic appetizers, perfect with cheeses, hummus, chopped tomatoes and basil, or anything that can be dipped, spread, or stacked. On its own, or with a pasta dish, it becomes one of those mini-vacations-in-Tuscany foods.

Years ago, when I was heading off to what was then the Soviet Union on a chefs' exchange, the Wheat Commission sent me a stack of recipe pamphlets titled "Ethnic Is Now," prepared by the Department of Agriculture. The pamphlets were poorly designed and graphically inept, the recipes were difficult to make sense of, and the instructions were so badly written that even as a professional chef I had a difficult time sorting out what they meant. Still, the recipes were intriguing. *Lavash* and other obscure Eastern European breads were listed, probably of no use to the Soviets but great for me. Then in the mid-nineties I was thrilled to discover bakers' olives in 10-pound tubs—good olives in scraps and pieces, already pitted and ready to go into bread dough. Still later, my friend Amelia Hard, one-time owner of Portland's Genoa restaurant and the doyenne of northern Italian cuisine, passed on a recipe for flatbread that used cornmeal. This recipe is a combination of all three influences.

1 tablespoon yeast
1½ cups warm water
1 tablespoon good-quality olive oil, plus more as needed
1 heaping teaspoon salt
3 cups unbleached white flour
1 cup cornmeal
1 cup chopped niçoise or kalamata olives

IN A LARGE BOWL or food processor, dissolve the yeast in ¾ cup of the warm water. Add the oil and salt. Blend or process in 1½ cups of the flour. If you are using a food processor, add the rest of the water with the motor running. Add the cornmeal and the remaining flour to obtain a very soft, pliable dough. If you are using a bowl, stir in the flour, cornmeal, and water to obtain the same results. Turn the dough on a floured surface, and sprinkle with the olives. Knead just enough to incorporate the olives. Oil the top of the dough and let rise for 45 minutes in a warm place.

PUNCH DOWN THE DOUGH and knead it for 2 minutes. Let rest for 2 minutes.

FORM THE DOUGH into 6 balls. (At this point it will keep for a week in the refrigerator.) Preheat the oven to 400°F. Flatten each ball of dough on a pizza pan or other flat pan, using the palm of your hand. A little oil will keep your hand from sticking to the dough. The thinner you flatten it, the better.

BAKE FOR 15 MINUTES, or until the dough is puffed and golden on the edges. Cut each round of flatbread into 8 wedges.

Makes 48 wedges

Hungarian Butterhorns

This recipe was dictated to me by my grandmother in the last months of her life. I have no idea why she wanted me to write it down, since I wasn't doing much cooking at the time and the recipe makes enough for sixty. Years later, I discovered it in my stack of recipes when I was looking for things to serve at brunch. The general consensus of my aunts is that "Hungarian" was added by my grandmother as a kind of joke, to give the pastry an exotic air, and that the true origin is probably the legendary Lottie Fraker, the cook at my grandmother's ranch for many years. The recipe is a farm classic in that it uses almost no ingredients yet it manages to deliver a crisp, tasty pastry with a minimum of butter and eggs.

For the Dough

> 4 cups unbleached white flour
> 1 teaspoon salt
> 1 tablespoon yeast
> 1¼ cups (2½ sticks) unsalted butter
> ½ cup sour cream
> 2 egg yolks (reserve the whites)

SIFT THE FLOUR and salt into a large bowl, add the yeast, then cut in the butter until the mixture is the consistency of coarse crumbs. Add the sour cream and egg yolks. Work the dough together until it forms a ball, and then let the dough rest for 5 minutes.

DIVIDE THE DOUGH into 8 balls, wrap, and chill for at least 2 hours or overnight.

Note: Double-wrapped dough will keep in the freezer for 2 months.

For the Filling

2 egg whites
2 tablespoons sugar
1 drop almond extract
¼ cup slivered almonds or other nuts

IN A MEDIUM BOWL, using an electric mixer, whip the egg whites until they form stiff peaks. Add the sugar, almond extract, and slivered almonds and whip just a bit more to combine.

To Assemble

1 cup powdered sugar for rolling and dusting

PREHEAT THE OVEN TO 400°F. Sprinkle the rolling surface with ½ cup of the powdered sugar. Roll out one of the balls of dough into a circle about ⅛ inch thick. Cut it into 8 wedges. Place a teaspoonful of the filling mixture onto the wide end of each piece. Roll toward the other, tapered point to form the horn. Repeat until the dough and meringue are gone.

BAKE ON A BUTTERED SHEET PAN for 10 to 12 minutes, until puffed and golden. Dust with the remaining ½ cup powdered sugar, and serve warm.

Makes 64 butterhorns

Shortbread

The buttery crunch of shortbread cookies is solace for just about any woe, plus shortbread is easy to make, keeps well, and elevates even the simplest bowl of ice cream. Some recipes call for special flours. I've eliminated them because I like the coarse crumb, and, besides, with the brown sugar it's going to be crumbly anyway. The secret in this recipe is the brown sugar, which gives a certain depth to the sweetness. The other secret is unsalted butter. If you haven't done so already, eliminate all salted butter from your repertoire now. For any kind of real cooking, you want to control the salt yourself. Once you're off the stuff, you will never understand how you put up with all that salt in the first place.

> *1½ cups (3 sticks) unsalted butter, at room temperature*
> *½ cup firmly packed brown sugar*
> *½ cup granulated sugar*
> *½ teaspoon salt*
> *1 teaspoon vanilla extract*
> *3 cups unbleached white flour*

IN A LARGE BOWL, using an electric mixer, cream together the butter and brown and granulated sugars until fluffy. Add the salt, vanilla, and flour and mix together thoroughly. Gather the dough into a ball and wrap in plastic. Chill for 4 to 6 hours.

ON A FLOURED SURFACE, roll out the dough to a thickness of ½ to ⅝ inch. Use a cookie cutter to cut out cookies, or cut the shortbread into pie-shaped wedges while still warm and let cool in the pan. Prick the shortbread with a fork and refrigerate it for 30 minutes or so.

Preheat the oven to 325°F. Bake the shortbread for 20 minutes, or until the cookies color slightly.

Makes 18 to 20 cookies

Variations

For almond shortbread, add 1 teaspoon almond extract.
For lemon shortbread, add the grated zest of 1 lemon.
For hazelnut shortbread, add ¾ cup skinned, crushed hazelnuts.

Chocolate Sauce

Making your own chocolate sauce is a soothing kitchen ritual. This sauce will keep almost forever in the fridge. It also makes a great gift. The amount of corn syrup can be adjusted to suit your tolerance for the fine flavor of bittersweet.

3 ounces bittersweet chocolate
1½ cups dark, unsweetened cocoa powder
½ cup espresso
½ cup brandy, water, or a flavored Torani syrup
1 tablespoon vanilla extract
2 cups light corn syrup

IN A DOUBLE BOILER, warm all the ingredients together. Let cook over rapidly boiling water for 1 minute while whisking briskly. Remove from the heat and allow to cool before refrigerating.

STORE IN THE REFRIGERATOR in a sealed container for up to 2 months. Serve at room temperature.

Makes about 3 cups

Raspberry Sauce

Raspberries are food of the gods, and preserving them for use when their short season is over is akin to a sacred act. Don't be fooled by those exorbitantly priced raspberries that appear in the market all winter long. They are imposters from South America, bred like tomatoes to live in cold storage and seduce the winter-weary. Instead, make and freeze this sauce, using the bounty of July and early August to cheer those bleak winter eves with the sublime deep scarlet ooze of last summer's berries. And it's easy.

> *2 pints raspberries*
> *1 tablespoon balsamic vinegar*
> *½ to 1 cup sugar*
> *3 drops orange-flower water*
> *1½ cups water*

PURÉE ALL THE INGREDIENTS in a food processor or blender. Adjust the amount of sugar according to the sweetness of the berries. Press the sauce through a China cap or other fine-mesh strainer with holes small enough to catch the seeds. Keep chilled.

THIS SAUCE WILL KEEP in the refrigerator for about 24 hours; after that, it will start to separate. It freezes well if sealed and wrapped.

Makes about 3 cups

Appetizers

Rocket Flatbread, Samish Bay Gouda

Chèvre Crackers, Herb Salsa

Mussel Sauté, Garden Lilies, and Curry

Morel Lasagna

Potato Horseradish Latkes, Smoked Salmon, Chive Cream

Crab Fondue, Fennel Breadsticks

Oyster Ouzo Cocktail

Salmon Caviar Spuds

Chanterelle Chive Toasts

Blue Cheesecake, Pear Flatbread

Singing Scallops Steamed, Sweet Cicely, Hard Cider

Halibut Cakes, Rouille

Oysters on the Half Shell, Cassis Mignonette Granita

Clams, Twigs, Lemon

Picnic Chicken Liver Terrine

Chanterelle Chive Toasts, page 50

Rocket Flatbread, Samish Bay Gouda

Arugula, otherwise known as rocket, has a spicy, nutty flavor that folks either love or hate. I love it. It is common now in the farmers' markets in the spring and fall. The heat of summer gives it a bitter, too hot flavor. The Samish Bay cheese is made by a dedicated farmer in the Skagit Valley of Washington State. His cows are fat and sassy and produce a rich, certified organic milk. Aging gives his cheeses a unique flavor. I prefer the Mont Blanchard, hard, aged, and crumbled—it's the perfect foil for the arugula.

> 1½ cups warm water
> 1 teaspoon salt
> ½ teaspoon yeast
> 3 tablespoons good-quality olive oil
> 3 to 3½ cups unbleached white flour
> 2 cups arugula leaves
> 1 cup caramelized onions (see the Chef's Tip)
> ½ cup roasted garlic cloves (see page 108)
> ½ teaspoon dried oregano
> 1 cup slivered, grated, or crumbled Samish Bay Gouda or other bold-
> flavored artisanal cheese

IN A LARGE BOWL, stir together the warm water, salt, yeast, and 1 tablespoon of the oil. Let sit for a few minutes until the yeast dissolves. Add the flour and stir, then turn out the contents of the bowl onto a floured surface and knead for just a minute, until the dough holds together. It will be sticky. Pour 1 tablespoon of the oil into a large bowl, then roll the ball of dough in it until coated. Let sit for 10 minutes. The dough will keep in the refrigerator for 3 days.

MEANWHILE, preheat the oven to 450°F. Toss the arugula and caramelized onions in a bowl with the remaining tablespoon of oil. Divide the dough into 2 pieces. In a shallow pan, flatten the dough, using the palm of your hand. Circle the dough with your hand, flattening it as you go. Do not pull it or tear it. Repeat with the remaining piece of dough. Cover the flat dough rounds with the oil-arugula-onion mixture and the garlic. Sprinkle with the oregano and cheese.

BAKE FOR 10 MINUTES, or until the dough puffs at the edges and turns golden. Cut into wedges and serve hot.

Note: The irregular shape and thickness are part of the rustic charm of this flatbread.

Makes six 6- to 8-inch round flatbreads

Chef's Tip: There are lots of ways to caramelize onions. Lazy girl that I am, I like to roast them in the oven. Preheat the oven to 350°F. Peel and slice the onions, any amount, and sprinkle with a few drops of vinegar and a tablespoon of sugar. This seasoning is more for voodoo, to encourage the onions to release their sugar, than anything else. Cover with foil and roast for 40 minutes or so, until the onions are soft and have colored at the edges. Remove the foil and return to the oven for 5 minutes, or until the onions turn slightly brown and finish carmelizing.

Chèvre Crackers, Herb Salsa

Homemade crackers are fun and easy to make. They can also transform a humble nibble into a festive and special appetizer. The really great thing about homemade crackers is that they can be made in any size— big triangles, cut with a knife, for dipping in hummus, or smaller bites cut with a favorite cookie cutter. One time, at the James Beard House in New York, we made little "Dungeness crab" crackers to float in the soup. Don't be too concerned about the type and amount of herbs in the salsa. The idea is to have lots of fresh green "herby" flavor.

For the Crackers

1 cup unbleached white flour
1 cup cake flour
¾ teaspoon salt
¾ teaspoon baking powder
2 tablespoons unsalted butter
2 tablespoons lard
¾ cup chèvre cheese
About ½ cup ice water

IN THE BOWL of a food processor, place the flours, salt, and baking powder. Pulse a few times to blend thoroughly. Add the butter, lard, and cheese and pulse again several times. The dough will be crumbly. With the motor running, add the ice water in drips until the dough forms a ball. Beat in the food processor for a few minutes before turning out onto a floured board. At this point, you can wrap the dough in plastic and refrigerate it for up to 4 days.

PREHEAT THE OVEN TO 350°F. To shape the crackers, roll out the dough very thin, about ⅛ inch. You can cut it with cookie cutters for special shapes, or cut the sheets into random shapes with a knife. Place the crackers on a baking sheet. Before baking, prick the crackers well with a fork. Bake for 20 minutes, until they have just a hint of pale color. Serve warm or store in an airtight jar for up to a week.

Note: The cracker dough can be carefully wrapped and frozen for up to a month.

Makes 2 or 3 dozen crackers

For the Salsa

> *2 cups chopped fresh herbs (at least 4 of the following: cilantro, Italian flat-leaf parsley, basil, mint, thyme, oregano, lovage, sweet cicely, sorrel)*
> *1 small cucumber, peeled, seeded, and cut into ⅛-inch dice*
> *1 tablespoon chopped chives*
> *2 tablespoons fruity extra virgin olive oil*
> *2 tablespoons red wine*
> *1 teaspoon grated lemon zest*
> *3 cloves garlic, finely chopped*
> *Salt and freshly ground black pepper*

MIX ALL INGREDIENTS in a nonreactive bowl. Chill for 20 minutes. Spoon over the crackers.

Makes about 3 cups

Chef's Tip: To keep herbs fresh, trim the bottom of the stem just a quarter inch or so to remove any brown or dried out parts, then keep the herbs in deep, cold water, either in or out of the refrigerator.

Mussel Sauté, Garden Lilies, and Curry

As a girl, I admired the deep blue sheen of the mussels clinging to the pilings just below the low-tide mark. When I asked my father why we didn't eat them, as we did the clams, he told me they were tough and nobody ate them. Like many from pioneer stock who had lived on a diet of foraged food when times were tough, my father's idea of a great meal was Châteaubriand and Bordeaux.

Everyone seems to prefer the big, juicy Mediterranean mussels, which have been grown in Puget Sound for several years now. However, any good mussels will do. Just make sure they close tight, and toss the ones with broken or cracked shells.

1 tablespoon curry powder
3 shallots, chopped
1 leek, chopped
1 large tomato, seeded and chopped
3 cloves garlic, crushed but whole
1 tablespoon good-quality olive oil
½ cup orange juice
½ cup white wine
2 tablespoons chopped chives
2 tablespoons chopped cilantro
2 quarts mussels, cleaned and debearded

IN A LARGE POT, add the curry powder, shallots, leek, tomato, and garlic to the olive oil and sauté over medium heat for 5 minutes, or until the shallots are soft and transparent. Add the orange juice, wine, half the chives, the cilantro, and the mussels. Cover and steam for 10 minutes, or until the shells open. Serve hot in bowls, garnished with the remaining chives.

Serves 6 as an appetizer or 4 as a main course

Morel Lasagna

On a good, wet day in late spring, at an altitude above sea level, in a patch of woods neither too bright nor too dark, under a patch of Douglas fir or maybe in an old burn, fungus royalty makes its stand. The morel is the great mushroom delicacy, abundant in the Northwest. There are good years and bad years for morels, and pickers never reveal exactly where their patches are. The dark, penetrating, slightly musty flavor is divine on its own, and Gorgonzola stands up to it just fine. Got a great red wine? Drink it with this.

For the Filling

4 leeks
2 tablespoons unsalted butter
4 cups fresh morel mushrooms
4 cloves garlic, finely minced
1 cup ricotta cheese
1 cup crumbled Gorgonzola or other blue cheese

IN A LARGE SAUTÉ PAN, sauté the leeks in 1 tablespoon of the butter until soft and translucent. Remove from the pan and set aside. In the same pan, sauté the morels with the garlic in the remaining tablespoon of butter. Set aside. With a large fork, blend the ricotta and crumbled blue cheese together in a small bowl and reserve.

For the Sauce

½ cup sherry vinegar
1 tablespoon finely diced shallot
1 teaspoon finely diced garlic
1 sprig fresh thyme
1 cup dry white wine

3 cups heavy cream
Salt and freshly ground black pepper

In a medium saucepan, boil the vinegar, shallot, garlic, and thyme until about 2 tablespoons of liquid remain. Add the white wine and boil until reduced by half. Add the cream and reduce by a third, until the mixture thickens and the bubbles on the surface are big. The sauce should be just thick enough to coat the back of a spoon. Season to taste with salt and pepper and reserve.

To Assemble

4 sheets of fresh pasta, each 8 by 8 inches (see page 194)
1 cup grated Parmigiano-Reggiano cheese

PREHEAT THE OVEN TO 350°F. Line the bottom of an 8- by 8-inch pan with a sheet of pasta. Overlap the pasta sheets if they aren't big enough to fit the pan. Spread the sautéed leeks on the sheet and drizzle with some of the sauce. Cover with a second sheet of pasta and fill with the sautéed morel mixture, reserving a few morels for the top. Drizzle the morels with some of the sauce. Cover with a third sheet of pasta. Spread with the ricotta–blue cheese mixture and top with the fourth sheet of pasta. Cover the top layer with the reserved morels and drizzle the remaining cream sauce over, then dust with the grated cheese. Bake for 35 minutes, until the top is bubbly and golden. Let the lasagna rest for 15 minutes or so before cutting. Serve warm.

Serves 8 as an appetizer or 6 as a main course

Potato Horseradish Latkes, Smoked Salmon, Chive Cream

I love these golden, crispy little cakes shiny with butter. Just a little horseradish gives them a friendly bite. I get my horseradish from my mother's garden, but you can find it fresh in any good produce market. Be careful with the heat: too much will bury the flavor of the smoked salmon. These latkes were made by my husband's grandmother, who came from a *shtetl* near Minsk at the turn of the last century with four small children in tow.

For the Latkes

4 medium potatoes, such as russets or Red Bliss
3 tablespoons chicken fat, lard, or butter
2 eggs, slightly beaten
1 heaping tablespoon prepared horseradish, or 1 teaspoon freshly grated
    horseradish
2 to 4 cloves garlic, finely chopped
½ teaspoon salt
½ cup peanut oil
4 ounces smoked salmon, broken into chunks

PEEL AND FINELY SHRED the potatoes. In a large mixing bowl, combine the potatoes with the chicken fat, eggs, horseradish, garlic, and salt. Mix well and shape into little patties, using about ½ cup of the potato mixture per patty. Chill the patties for 15 minutes. Coat the bottom of a large sauté pan with oil, and heat over medium-high heat until the oil is hot. Fry the latkes for 2 minutes per side, until crispy and golden. Serve topped with chunks of smoked salmon and a dollop of chive cream (recipe follows).

For the Chive Cream

> *1 cup sour cream*
> *¼ cup finely minced chives*

MIX the sour cream and chives together.

Serves 4 to 6 as an appetizer

Crab Fondue, Fennel Breadsticks

The Goose Hollow Inn is a famous Portland watering hole. In the early seventies it was the hangout for an eclectic bunch of local personalities. Artists, various miscreants, winos, politicos, warmongers and protesters, celebrities and stoners—all rubbed shoulders in the crammed, smoke-filled rooms. The owner, in fact, later became Portland's mayor. On Fridays the inn served a cheddar-and-crab sandwich, a gooey match made in heaven and, as it turns out, inspiration for a fondue. We serve it with the breadsticks we make every day for our breadbasket at the restaurant.

> *1 cup good spicy dry white wine, such as Gewürztraminer or Riesling*
> *8 ounces Emmenthaler or other Swiss cheese, cut into chunks*
> *8 ounces Gruyère cheese, cut into chunks*
> *1 tablespoon unbleached white flour*
> *1 cup Dungeness crabmeat*
> *2 tablespoons dry sherry*
> *Fennel Breadsticks (see page 19)*

PUT THE WHITE WINE, crabmeat and cheeses in a medium saucepan and heat slowly over medium heat, stirring until the cheeses are melted and the mixture is thick and creamy. Add the flour and whisk, then add the sherry. Keep warm over low heat until ready to use.

SERVE IN A CHAFING DISH or a little pot warmed by a candle. Use the breadsticks for dipping.

Note: This does not reheat well.

Serves 4 as an appetizer

Oysters

DURING THE GOLDEN AGE OF THE OYSTER, YOU COULD EAT THEM OFF the half shell at the Greengage Saloon in Rawlins, Wyoming. In Portland, Oregon, ladies in hats and gloves spooned "potage" at Dan and Louis Oyster House. In Montana, the oysters came off the train in Missoula packed in big wooden barrels layered in sawdust and ice, and in a mining town in Nevada a doomed man left his imprint on the culinary world forever when he ordered for his last meal fried oysters and eggs—still served as Hangtown Fry. At Delmonico's, the fabled Manhattan restaurant of the last century, Diamond Jim Brady ate twenty dozen oysters at the beginning of a meal that included a baron of beef, pheasant, and several bottles of Champagne, cementing his legend as a gourmand and glutton. They say he did live to dine again, and that he liked oysters very much. ▮▮ OYSTERS ARE AN ACQUIRED TASTE. My brothers and I would watch in disgust, making big *ick* sounds, as our folks slurped the slimy orbs down. My parents hooted with laughter and assured us that someday we too would eat oysters. I was a vision of nonchalance when I downed my first oyster at a party in Gearhart, Oregon. As an eighteen-year-old art student, I was out to impress my companion, a painter of some repute. The host, who later became a famous foodie, proffered the tray at just the right moment. I took a sip of the glorious Mersault, upended the shell, and tried to slurp delicately as I had seen my mother

<SHIP'S CABIN — "DAN & LOUIS OYSTER BAR" — 208 S.W. ANKENY, PORTLAND, ORE.>

Dan & Louis Oyster Bar in Portland, Oregon, has been serving oysters for over a hundred years.

do countless times. The oyster slid into my mouth, whole, soft, and fat. As I chewed and swallowed, a cacophony of texture and flavor lit up my palate. The slug of Mersault I downed, in a pathetic attempt to regain my composure, just exalted the flavor rolling around in my mouth. I was hooked. IN THE THIRTY YEARS SINCE THEN, I have eaten oysters everywhere. In 1988 I took several dozen Judd Cove oysters, from our local farm, to Moscow. The Russians looked at them in wonder, as if they were moon rocks. It was only later I learned that oysters, along with tuxedos and golf, were regarded as the epitome of capitalist decadence. At Hemingway's old haunt, the Closerie des Lilas in Paris, my mom and I dined on the *plateau prestige,* a three-story affair consisting of ten different kinds of oysters from the famous beds of France, where all the oysters have place names like wines. At the Acme Oyster Bar in New Orleans, they serve the po' boy: oysters, breaded, deep-fried, and crunchy, on a soft, white roll with homemade mayonnaise. At the Oyster Bar in Manhattan's Grand Central Terminal, if you land at the right time of year, thirty different oysters are on the menu from all across the country and Canada too. THE BEST OYSTERS IN THE WORLD come from my islands, the San Juans of northwestern Washington. Our cold, clear sound with its mix of fresh water and salt water, and little wave action, is the perfect habitat for them. The Pacific oyster *(Crassostrea gigas)* is a native of Japan, brought here after the decimation of the native oyster, the tiny Olympia *(Ostrea lurida).* Now the Pacific has naturalized, and oysters found in the wild are likely Pacifics. Interestingly enough, the eastern or Atlantic oyster *(Crassostrea virginica)* doesn't grow or reproduce in West Coast waters. █▐▌█ THE OLD SAW ABOUT EATING OYSTERS only in a month with an *R* in it comes from the days before refrigeration and modern oyster-farming techniques. Today, oysters can be eaten year-round, even though they go soft during their reproductive cycle. Oyster farmers have figured out how to interrupt this cycle by moving them to cold water, since the cycle begins

THIS LOCATION FOR 34 YEARS

AMERICAN OYSTER HOUSE
1512 WESTLAKE AVE.
NEAR 4TH AND PIKE
SEATTLE

A. H. SUDDRETH   MAIN 5273

1942

when the water warms, usually just a matter of a few degrees. Naturally enough, this warming happens in the summer—note the lack of an *R* in the months of May through August. Wild oysters become milky and soft and are not at their best during the warmer months unless they have been moved to cold, deep water. Oysters have been farmed this way in the Pacific Northwest for the past century.

Oyster Ouzo Cocktail

Let's get this straight right away. I am not a fan of cocktail sauce. I really don't like burny, hot food. I don't believe hot peppers really make anything taste better. Slathering on the barbecue sauce or dousing beautiful food with Tabasco is my idea of desecration. Didn't we learn in fifth grade that Columbus searched for the New World so he could find pepper, the most desired of all the spices, because it was needed to cover the flavor of meat past its prime? All this being said, here is a recipe for something akin to cocktail sauce, and, horror of horrors, it goes on oysters! Nonetheless, I love my customers and they kept asking for a sauce, so here it is. It's perfect for a dinner party because you can make it in advance and stash it in the fridge.

Note: Any sexy, dramatic glasses will do for serving.

> 18 fresh yearling oysters, shucked (see the Chef's Tip on page 64), or substitute Dungeness crabmeat.
> 1½ cups House Ketchup (see page 2)
> Juice and grated zest of 1 lemon
> 1 teaspoon freshly grated horseradish, or 1 tablespoon prepared horseradish
> 3 ounces ouzo, Pernod, sambuca, or other anise-flavored liqueur
> 2 cups torn, mild-flavored lettuce leaves, such as Bibb or iceberg
> Lime wedges and chives for garnish

KEEP THE OYSTERS REFRIGERATED until ready to serve. In a medium bowl, whisk together the ketchup, lemon juice and zest, horseradish, and ouzo and set aside. Fill each serving glass a quarter full with the chopped lettuce, add a tablespoon of cocktail sauce, top with 3 oysters and another good dollop of sauce, and finally garnish with lime wedges and chives. Serve chilled.

Serves 6 as an appetizer

Salmon Caviar Spuds

Let's face it, caviar is the ultimate appetizer. Too bad so few of us can indulge in it. Too bad, too, if you don't like the lovely little eggs—that just means more for me. I counted up my major caviar episodes, and to my delight there are more than a few. I have been blessed to be in the right place at the right time. The first time I had caviar was in the south of France with "the last of the millionaire playboys" (I hear there is a whole new crop now). It was overload—too much of everything—and I can look back now and see that he was just showing off, and my memory is blurred with twinkly lights, the warm breeze, and the luscious scent of Macanudos. Twenty years later I sat in a steamy Moscow restaurant kitchen, The Storks, with Wayne Ludvigsen and Neal Roseman and watched in astonishment as a battered metal 2-quart bowl of caviar with a soup spoon sticking out of it was unceremoniously plopped down in front of us, along with a stack of little buckwheat cakes. That was breakfast, on our first day as part of a chefs' exchange. It was just as Joan Jernigan, owner of the Duck Soup Inn, had told me, "You won't make any money in the restaurant biz, but you will live really well."

Potatoes are graded by size. "C"s are the smallest I've seen. Talk to your produce vendor; they will be happy to get you some. This dish is wonderfully simple, and you can use as much or as little caviar as you like.

> 1 tablespoon salt
> 24 small fingerling potatoes or tiny Red Bliss potatoes
> 1 cup sour cream
> 4 ounces salmon caviar
> Chopped chives for garnish

FILL A MEDIUM SAUCEPAN two-thirds full with water. Add the salt and potatoes. Place over high heat and bring to a boil, then lower the heat and simmer for 8 to 10 minutes, or until the potatoes are tender. Drain and chill the potatoes.

TO SERVE, cut a sliver off the bottom of each potato so it will sit flat. Pare a slightly larger piece off the top. Place a small dollop of sour cream on top. Spoon the salmon caviar onto the sour cream and garnish with the chives. Serve cold.

Serves 10 to 12 as an appetizer

Chanterelle Chive Toasts

What to do with the permanent starlet of mushrooms, revered the world over for its rich, buttery yet slightly tart flavor? Chanterelles are great with salmon and chicken, in soups, and with noodles. When they first arrive at our kitchen door in the fall, usually very late in the afternoon, it is just beginning to get dark outside. The restaurant kitchen is all steamed up and we are just seating our first tables. I can't wait for the next day to serve them. Fortunately, I always have fresh chives and lots of butter.

For the Mushrooms

1 pound chanterelle mushrooms
3 tablespoons unsalted butter
4 to 6 cloves garlic, crushed
¼ cup soft white wine
1 tablespoon chopped fresh thyme leaves
2 tablespoons chopped Italian flat-leaf parsley
2 tablespoons chopped chives

PICK THROUGH THE CHANTERELLES to remove fir needles, twigs, and forest fuzz. Brush gently; do not wash them. Tear the larger mushrooms into quarters or thirds. Leave small mushrooms whole.

IN A WIDE SAUTÉ PAN, melt the butter with the garlic over medium heat and allow the flavors to blend for a few minutes, then add the mushrooms and turn up the heat. Sauté over high heat for 3 minutes or so, until the mushrooms start to soften and release their juice. Add the wine and thyme and continue to sauté for a few minutes more, until the wine reduces and the thyme releases its aroma. Turn off the heat and add the parsley and chives.

SERVE ON TOASTS (recipe follows), hot or warm, within half an hour.

For the Toasts

18 slices baguette
Unsalted butter, melted, for brushing

PREHEAT THE OVEN TO 450°F. Brush both sides of the baguette slices with the melted butter and toast on a sheet pan for 4 minutes on each side, or until just golden. Top each slice with a spoonful of the sautéed mushroom mixture and serve.

Serves 6 as an appetizer

Champagne

WHEN I DINE OUT, I ALWAYS ORDER CHAMPAGNE FIRST. EVEN IF IT'S just a glass of the house pour, it gives me something to do while I get settled and start perusing the menu. Also, it allows me to spend some time with the wine list. Wine lists can be a novel, a geography trip, heartburn, or a snooze. Never be intimidated by a wine steward; most are learning on the job. The few who do have wine savvy are genuinely eager to share their knowledge and turn people on to wine. I always ask questions: What are their favorites on the list? Do they approve of pinot noir with salmon? Their answers tell me just how knowledgeable they are. And if the list is boring or too expensive or poorly spelled, disorganized, too cutesy, or, worst of all, divided by flavors ("The Bold," "The Beautiful"!), I will order Champagne. In the worst places you can at least trust a bottle of Champagne, and in the best places you are putting your hosts on notice. You are saying, "We are here to enjoy ourselves. We want to have some good fun and some good food. We expect you to take care of us in your very best manner, and we trust you to do so." This signal allows the serving team to do their best work. Word will drift into the kitchen. Little treats might appear. In France, the head waiter will come to take your order. At Tour d'Argent in Paris, you might be invited to tour the wine cellar. If nothing at all happens, we still have our frothy, festive moment when the glasses bubble and time stops and we are young and beautiful and everything is right in the world. **[10:11]** EVERYONE LOVES CHAMPAGNE FOR ITS FINE, FRIENDLY, AND ELEGANT FLAVOR—and, of course, for the bubbles. Champagne goes with everything: roast beef, caviar, even corn dogs. Better still, it goes with nothing at all. Real Champagne comes from the region of Champagne northeast of Paris. All the others—those from Spain, California, Italy, or Australia—are just sparkling wines. Some of these sparklers are world-class and every bit as amiable as real Champagne; however, they are *not* Champagne. None have the history or romance of the great French Champagne houses, where whole towns are literally built on the Champagne business. **[10:11]** MORE THAN FORTY MILES OF LIMESTONE CAVES run under the French town of Epernay, complete with caverns, entrances and exits, secret passages, and dead ends. In the winter, when the tourist hordes are absent, one is allowed a "self-guided" tour of the cellars. In 1986 I spent a day wandering the cellars of Dom Perignon. On the steps to the caves there is a memorial to the employees of Dom Perignon who "died for France," among them the director, a woman who was "deported" after the Gestapo discovered that Dom was hiding hundreds of Jews in the cellars. This history lesson was coupled with my discovery of two happy Frenchmen in hip waders running the bottling machine, singing, with the radio on at full volume, John Lennon's "Imagine" while awash in a sea of Champagne that swirled around the floor, the pungent odor of the bubbles and limestone filling the air, the rattle of the bottling machine as the backbeat, the evident centuries of joy and sadness everywhere.

Blue Cheesecake, Pear Flatbread

In the early days of the restaurant, I was looking for tasty, unusual starters that weren't too complicated to plate and serve. My kitchen staff usually consisted of a local high schooler who doubled as a dishwasher and liked the free meal at the end of the night. I was making lots of cheesecakes for desserts, and naturally I thought I was a genius for inventing this savory version. Just about the same time, cheese terrines, loafs, and cakes started appearing on restaurant menus around the country. However, I felt a certain satisfaction and pride when the recipe that appeared in a national food publication didn't turn out as rich and light as mine. It's perfect for an appetizer buffet and can be frozen for up to a month; just be sure to let it thaw in the refrigerator for two days. The other secret is that you can substitute almost any kind of semisoft cheese for the blue cheese.

For the Crust

> 1 cup bread crumbs
> 1½ teaspoons unbleached white flour
> ¼ cup grated Parmesan cheese
> ⅓ cup unsalted butter, melted

BLEND ALL THE INGREDIENTS in a bowl or food processor until crumbly and soft. Pat the crust into the bottom of a 6-inch springform pan. Chill for 10 minutes. Meanwhile, preheat the oven to 375°F.

For the Filling

> 12 ounces good-quality blue cheese, such as Oregon Blue, Gorgonzola, or Maytag, at room temperature
> 12 ounces cream cheese, at room temperature

1 tablespoon unbleached white flour
3 eggs
¾ cup sour cream

IN A LARGE MIXING BOWL, using an electric mixer, blend the blue cheese, cream cheese, and flour. Add the eggs, one at a time, beating until well blended. Do not overbeat or the cheesecake will puff up and crack while baking.

POUR THE CHEESE MIXTURE into the prepared crust, and wrap the outside of the pan with foil to prevent leaks. Bake in a *bain-marie* (see the Chef's Tip) for 1 hour and 10 minutes.

TURN THE OVEN OFF. Spread the top of the cheesecake with the sour cream, and then leave the cake in the oven, with the door open a bit, to settle for 1 hour. Place the cheesecake, still in its springform pan, in the refrigerator overnight to chill.

WHEN READY TO SERVE, remove from the pan, and cut the cheese-cake into wedges. Serve with the pear flatbread (recipe follows).

Serves 10 as an appetizer

For the Flatbread

1 teaspoon yeast
1 cup warm water
1 teaspoon salt
2 tablespoons good-quality olive oil
¼ cup chopped, toasted walnuts
¾ cup chopped dried pear
1½ cups unbleached white flour

IN A MEDIUM BOWL, add the yeast to the water and salt and let sit for a few minutes. Add the olive oil, walnuts, and pear and stir to blend. Stir in the flour and then knead for 1 minute. Let rest for 30 minutes.

PREHEAT THE OVEN TO 450°F. Oil a baking sheet. Divide the dough into 4 pieces. Roll each piece out ¼ to ½ inch thick on the baking sheet and bake for 7 minutes. The flatbreads can be any shape that fits your pan.

Chef's Tip: A *bain-marie*—literally "Marie's bath"—is a cooking technique in which a roasting pan containing a few inches of water holds whatever is baking or roasting. In the case of a cheesecake, the water surrounding the cake keeps the temperature steady and prevents a crust from forming on the outside. (It also works well for custards, flans, and delicate cakes.) I wrap the bottom of the cheesecake pan in foil to keep the water out before I place it in the empty roasting pan, and then I fill the roasting pan with cool water until it comes halfway up the side of the cheesecake. Then the roasting pan and water go carefully into the oven.

Singing Scallops Steamed, Sweet Cicely, Hard Cider

Chuck is the Indian word for water. I grew up hearing the term "salt chuck": don't fall in it; look what we pulled out of it. The Haida, the Lummi, the Samish, and the Swinomish all fished, foraged, and camped in the San Juan Islands. The beach that runs along the road in Westsound on Orcas Island is called Picnic Beach in honor of the Lummis who used to come and stay every summer to pick berries, smoke oysters and clams, and dry fish. The native pink scallops were a rare treat because they live so deep in the chuck. Today, divers chase them across the bottom, where they sprint by expelling water for propulsion.

> 2 tablespoons chopped garlic
> 4 green onions, finely chopped
> ½ fennel bulb, thinly sliced
> ½ cup extra virgin olive oil
> 1½ cups hard cider
> ½ cup finely chopped fennel fronds
> 4 stems sweet cicely, coarsely chopped
> 1 quart live scallops in the shell, about 2½ pounds

IN A LARGE SAUCEPAN, sauté the garlic, onions, and fennel bulb in the oil over medium heat until they are soft and translucent, 7 to 8 minutes or so. Add the cider, chopped fronds, and sweet cicely, along with the scallops. Cover with a tight-fitting lid, turn the heat to high, and steam the scallops until the shells open wide and the scallops look firm and plump. Serve immediately.

Serves 4 as an appetizer

Halibut Cakes, Rouille

The secret ingredient in these cakes is crab—but just a little. The cakes really benefit when the sweet pepper and onion are cooked before they go into the mix. The texture is more consistent, and the cakes are moist and tender.

For the Halibut Cakes

2 cups halibut trim and tails (ask your fishmonger), cut into ½-inch dice
*   *or coarsely ground in a food processor*
½ cup crabmeat, crumbled
½ cup mayonnaise, homemade (see page 8) or purchased
½ teaspoon salt
1 teaspoon freshly ground black pepper
½ cup chopped Italian flat-leaf parsley
1 tablespoon butter
3 shallots, finely diced
4 cloves garlic, finely minced
½ red bell pepper, finely diced
½ cup bread crumbs
1 egg
1 tablespoon peanut oil

IN A MEDIUM BOWL, combine the halibut, crabmeat, mayonnaise, salt, pepper, and parsley. Mix lightly and refrigerate.

MEANWHILE, in a medium sauté pan, add butter and sauté the shallots, garlic, and red pepper for 5 minutes or so, until translucent and soft. Let cool for a few minutes, then add to the halibut mixture. Blend well, then add the bread crumbs and egg. Blend well again.

USING ABOUT A QUARTER of a cup for each, shape the mixture into cakes, place in a sheet pan, and chill. Let set for at least 4 hours or overnight.

IN A LARGE SAUTÉ PAN, heat oil over medium heat and sauté the cakes for 4 minutes per side, or until golden and crispy. Serve immediately, with a dollop of rouille (recipe follows) on top.

Makes about 16 cakes

For the Rouille

1 egg
1 egg yolk
2 cloves garlic
½ red bell pepper
½ cup bread crumbs
⅓ cup red wine vinegar
1 small dried red chili
1 cup good-quality olive oil
Salt and freshly ground black pepper

PLACE THE EGG, egg yolk, garlic, bell pepper, bread crumbs, vinegar, and dried red chili in a food processor and process until smooth. Add the oil in a slow, steady stream until the egg emulsifies and the rouille stiffens. Season with salt and pepper to taste. It will keep in a sealed container in the refrigerator for 1 week.

Makes about 1½ cups

Chef's Tip: There has been a lot of fuss lately about raw eggs. This concern arises from the ugly salmonella bacteria that move themselves around the planet in and on eggs. They can be eliminated by wiping eggs carefully with a 1 percent bleach solution. This is flavorless and quite safe. There is no cure for salmonella actually in the egg. But comfort yourself with these facts: salmonella shows up in one out of every ten thousand eggs. A commercial laying hen may lay only three hundred eggs or so in her career, and even if infected she may never lay an egg with salmonella in it. Interestingly enough, acid also kills germs.

Oysters on the Half Shell, Cassis Mignonette Granita

Here is another idea that spread through the culinary world like wildfire. Only this is the version I am taking credit for. I know there is no new food. Naturally, I'm discounting anything that's bioengineered, genetically mutated, or cobbled together from petroleum by-products. The ancient Roman texts, medieval books, early twentieth-century cookbooks—somewhere, in some way, all have ultimately used every flavor combination there is. But new techniques are always created with each new kitchen toy.

Mignonette is a classic French accompaniment for shellfish. I had been worrying that the oysters would not be cold enough at the table, and I was inspired in a dream to freeze the granita, Italian style. The formula for mignonette is simple. The wines and vinegars can be mixed and matched. Have at it. You too can be a culinary innovator.

½ cup currant vinegar
½ cup off-dry white wine, such as Riesling or Gewürztraminer
¼ cup cassis
1 tablespoon finely minced shallot
20 black peppercorns
24 top-quality, fresh-from-the-sea yearling oysters, shucked (see the Chef's Tip) and chilled
Lemon or lime wedges (optional)

IN A SMALL BOWL, whisk together the vinegar, wine, cassis, shallot, and peppercorns. Freeze in a shallow pan, stirring occasionally, for several hours. Use a heavy spoon to scrape the resulting ice into 6 small ramekins. To serve, place 4 oysters on each plate, with ice and a ramekin of the granita. Garnish with wedges of lemon or lime if you like.

Serves 6 as an appetizer

Chef's Tip: To shuck an oyster, hold the oyster with a towel on a flat, hard surface. Leave the hinge end exposed. Find, by gently wiggling the tip of your oyster knife, the crevice at the hinge end. With a brusque move, insert the knife at least ¼ inch. Using leverage, turn the knife 150 degrees until it pries open the oyster. At this point, let the knife flatten again, move the knife under the shell over the surface of the meat, and cut the abductor muscle (visualizing the hinge as 12 o'clock, the muscle is always at 8 o'clock). As soon as that muscle is cut, the entire top of the oyster shell should slide off. Cut the same muscle underneath the flesh, wipe out any bits of broken shell that have collected around the edge, and voilà! Oyster on the half shell.

Clams, Twigs, Lemon

I make this with the little manila clams I get from my fishmonger. My theory is, the bigger the clams are, the quicker they get tough. This is definitely a dish for little clams. The amount of garlic is, as usual, extremely flexible. Garlic is always iffy because the flavor of each individual bulb varies according to the amount of sun and water it received while growing, the soil it was grown in, the way it was harvested and stored, the season, and even the variety of garlic. Combine these variables with your eaters' penchant for garlic and you come up with recipes that call for 5 to 20 cloves of garlic. Use a little or a lot. It's all good.

> *1 quart steamer or other small clams, scrubbed and rinsed*
> *6 shallots, sliced in thin wedges*
> *10 cloves garlic, crushed*
> *1 cup (2 sticks) unsalted butter, melted*
> *10 sprigs Italian flat-leaf parsley, coarsely chopped*
> *6 stems thyme leaf*
> *6 stems marjoram*
> *Grated zest of 1 lemon*
> *⅓ cup white wine*
> *½ cup lemon vodka*
> *Freshly ground black pepper*
> *Salt*

PLACE ALL THE INGREDIENTS in a large pot with a tight-fitting lid. Make sure the shallots and garlic are on the bottom of the pan, in the butter. Bring the mixture to a boil and steam until the clams have opened and released their liquor, about 10 minutes. Taste the broth and adjust the seasoning with more salt and pepper if you like. Serve hot.

Serves 4 as an appetizer or 2 as a main course

Picnic Chicken Liver Terrine

Twenty-five years ago, pâtés and terrines were very popular on restaurant menus. I suspect that those of us who cooked were thrilled to finally be able to make all these dishes that, before the availability of the Cuisinart, involved hours of kitchen drudgery.

> *1 cup pale dry sherry*
> *½ cup beef stock*
> *1 teaspoon freshly ground black pepper*
> *4 shallots, chopped*
> *1 pound chicken livers*
> *½ cup (1 stick) unsalted butter, at room temperature*
> *Salt*
> *½ cup heavy cream, whipped*
> *1 tablespoon unflavored gelatin*
> *1 egg white*

IN A LARGE, SHALLOW SKILLET, bring the sherry, stock, and pepper to a simmer. Add the shallots and chicken livers and simmer for 5 minutes. Turn off the heat and let cool for 10 minutes.

STRAIN THE LIVERS and shallots from the broth, reserving the broth, and cool to room temperature.

PURÉE THE LIVERS and cooked shallots in a food processor with the butter until perfectly smooth. Add salt to taste. Place the mixture in a large bowl and fold in the whipped cream. Spoon the entire mixture into an attractive loaf pan, approximately 1 quart in capacity, and chill. Make sure you have at least half an inch to spare around the rim.

MEANWHILE, in a small saucepan over medium heat, heat the reserved broth with the gelatin. When the liquid begins to simmer, add the egg white, whisking constantly until a "raft" forms on the surface. Use a flat spoon to collect and discard the foam. Strain the liquid through cheesecloth and discard the solids. You should have about ¾ cup of clear broth. Let it cool slightly, but pour it onto the top of the chilled terrine while still liquid. Refrigerate overnight.

SERVE COLD IN THE PAN with baguettes or crackers.

Serves 10 as an appetizer

Salads

Bibb, Beets, Balsamico, Bermuda Triangle

Smoked Salmon, Arugula, Fingerling Chips

Roasted Vegetable Salad, Tomato Caper Vinaigrette

Heirloom Garden Tomatoes, Walnut Basil Dressing

Spring Herb Salad, Grilled Lamb, Feta Eggplant Baba Ghanoush

Grilled Asparagus, Bresaola, Shaved Parmesan

Classic Duck Salad

My Granny's Winter Salad

Poached Salmon, Lemon Ginger Aïoli

Fennel, Parmesan, Zested Lemon Vinaigrette

Grilled Ahi Niçoise, Pea Shoots, Wrinkled Olive Tapenade

Bibb, Beets, Balsamico, Bermuda Triangle

This is a very simple salad that depends solely on the quality of the ingredients. More than just cheese poetry, the aged goat cheese called Bermuda Triangle, from Cypress Grove, is truly, as the label claims, a flavor to get lost in. Our beets come from Horse-Drawn Farm on Lopez Island. They are perfect candidates for roasting. The crunch of the Bibb lettuce and its nonassertive flavor allow the flavor of the cheese and the beets to cheer us with their boldness. And all these ingredients are available in the middle of winter, when gardens lie fallow and gardeners snooze.

For the Beets

2 medium beets

PREHEAT THE OVEN TO 350°F. Wrap the beets in foil and roast them in the oven for 40 minutes or so, until tender. This step can be done in advance, and the beets can be refrigerated for up to 3 days. When cooled, peel the beets by rubbing the skin off under cold running water.

For the Dressing

⅓ cup balsamic vinegar
1 cup olive oil
½ teaspoon salt
A few grinds of black pepper

IN A MEDIUM BOWL, whisk all the ingredients together. The dressing will keep in the refrigerator for weeks.

To Assemble

1 large head red Bibb lettuce, separated, washed, and torn into bite-size pieces

6 to 8 ounces Bermuda Triangle or other aged goat cheese

SLICE THE BEETS and place in a large bowl with the greens. Toss with enough of the dressing to moisten the greens and the beets. Arrange on the plate with the cheese on the side. Serve immediately.

Serves 6

Smoked Salmon, Arugula, Fingerling Chips

This is one of those salads that could almost be a meal. At Christina's we always have at least one substantial salad on the menu besides the house salad. Definitely a fall and winter concoction, this one is fairly elaborate to make, but if you want to dine on a meaningful salad, this is it. The moist smoked salmon is a great foil for the fingerling potatoes in their swath of capers and olive oil.

For the Dressing

⅓ cup sherry vinegar
1 tablespoon caper juice
1½ teaspoons Dijon mustard
1 teaspoon sugar
1 cup olive oil
Salt and freshly ground black pepper

IN A MEDIUM BOWL, whisk all the ingredients together.

For the Chips

¾ cup peanut oil for frying
2 uncooked fingerling potatoes, thinly sliced and soaked in cold water

HEAT THE PEANUT OIL in a deep saucepan over high heat to 365°F. Drain the potato slices and dry thoroughly. Fry in the oil, in batches if necessary. Remove from the oil with a slotted spoon and drain on paper towels.

To Assemble

> 6 to 8 whole, cooked Tom Thumb or Russian fingerling or other small,
> flavorful potatoes
> 6 ounces smoked salmon, broken into large chunks
> ½ red onion, sliced thin
> ¼ cup chopped parsley
> 1 tablespoon capers
> 6 cups loosely packed arugula leaves

CUT THE POTATOES IN HALF lengthwise, if necessary, and in a small bowl toss them with the smoked salmon, onion, parsley, capers, and half of the dressing until thoroughly moistened. Refrigerate the rest of the dressing for another use. Toss the arugula with the chips. Place the smoked salmon and potato mixture on a plate. Top with the greens and chip mixture. Serve immediately.

Serves 6

Roasted Vegetable Salad, Tomato Caper Vinaigrette

Chefs, like all who cook, have their stalwarts: favorite ingredients, tried-and-true flavors with a universal appeal. When summer comes, roasted vegetables are one of mine. Nothing is more delicious than toothsome garden vegetables drizzled with olive oil and a few herbs and heated just enough to release the flavors. Eat them late on a summer afternoon with a bunch of friends outdoors, with a brave little red wine and some grilled fish. I like to cut the vegetables in different ways to accentuate their color. Just be sure to keep them the same thickness so they are done at the same time. One exception is the onions. Cut them thinner.

For the Vegetables

5 zucchini
4 summer squash
2 red bell peppers
1 red onion
3 tablespoons olive oil
3 cloves garlic, very finely minced
1 teaspoon salt
½ cup chopped fresh basil

TRIM THE STEM ENDS from the zucchini and cut them lengthwise into 3 or 4 pieces. Cut these in half. Trim the ends from the summer squash and slice them in rounds about ¼ inch thick. Core and seed the peppers and cut them into strips, starting at the stem end. Peel the red onion, leaving the root end intact. Cut the onion in half directly through the middle of the root end. Then cut it into wedges, leaving a piece of the root intact. This technique will hold the onion wedge together through the roasting.

TOSS ALL THE VEGETABLES in a bowl with the olive oil, garlic, and salt. Place in a large pan and roast in a 400°F oven for 12 to 14 minutes until tender. Remove from the heat to a large platter. Sprinkle with the chopped basil and toss gently. The vegetables will continue to cook as they cool.

For the Dressing

1 garden-ripe tomato, seeded and chopped
1 tablespoon best-quality red wine vinegar
1 tablespoon capers with their juice
⅓ cup extra virgin olive oil
1 tablespoon chopped parsley
Salt and freshly ground black pepper

IN A MEDIUM BOWL, whisk together all the ingredients.

To Assemble

DRIZZLE THE DRESSING over the vegetables. Serve warm or at room temperature.

Serves 6

Tomatoes

LATE SUMMER IS THE TIME TO EAT TOMATOES. IF YOU ARE CLEVER and talented, you may be getting them from your own garden. Lucky you. The warm days of August are the perfect time to stroll through the garden with a salt shaker and eat those little Sweet 100s right off the vine. For the rest of us, the black-thumb crowd (or is it just the microclimate of our particular garden plot?), we have to do some other kind of work to get seriously perfect and wonderful garden-ripe tomatoes. First try family, neighbors, friends, and distant relatives. Some of them may be gifted growers of tomatoes. Cultivate them. Most people want to pitch movie ideas to my friend the Hollywood producer. All I want is her tomatoes. She has ripe tomatoes a month earlier than everyone else! Beefsteak, Big Boy, Brandywine, Mr. Stripey, Bob's Favorite: these varieties are so beautiful, with their deep colors and knobby stems. ▨ THE NEXT BEST HOPE FOR GOOD TOMATOES is the farmers' market. Practically every community has one these days. Seek one out and you will be well rewarded. Devoted gardeners become serious farmers with help and encouragement from those of us who like to eat. The tender lettuces, tiny sweet carrots, beets, melons, and squash taste nothing like their supermarket counterparts. If you haven't sampled these market wares, may I suggest you immediately attend the Saturday (usually) farmers' market and buy, buy, buy. There is nothing so inspiring to someone who likes to cook as a bag of goodies from someone's lovingly tended, hopefully organic garden. When produce is this fresh it requires little in the way of embellishment to make it superb.

I HAVE A WEAKNESS FOR TOMATO SANDWICHES. Slather fresh white bread with mayonnaise, cover with thick slices of garden-ripe tomato warm from the garden, and mash another piece of bread on top to hold it together. Tuck a big napkin under your chin to catch the drips.

Tomato lover's garden.

Here's another one: grilled sharp cheddar cheese sandwiches with bacon and slices of tomato. If you eat many of these, you could be making friends with a heart surgeon, but it may be worth it. You decide.

Heirloom Garden Tomatoes, Walnut Basil Dressing

My girlfriend, the movie "mogul," is a dedicated tomato farmer. Her public persona is that of a hugely successful movie producer, but in her private life she's a gardener with a penchant for tomatoes. She knows all the varieties—which ones are good in pots, which ripen sooner than later. She created a trellised and bountiful vegetable garden on Orcas Island so she could sit with her friends on a bench in the corner and eat tomatoes warm from the sun while cicadas buzz and the madrona bark curls up in the breeze.

This version of the classic "caprese" is only worth making when there are real ripe garden tomatoes available.

For the Dressing

⅓ cup white balsamic vinegar
1 cup good-quality or extra virgin olive oil
1 tablespoon finely chopped fresh basil
1 cup walnut oil

IN A MEDIUM BOWL, whisk all the ingredients together.

To Assemble

6 heirloom tomatoes of various types (1 per serving)
3 balls buffalo mozzarella, about 4 ounces
24 whole basil leaves
1 pint cherry tomatoes of various types
Freshly ground black pepper

CORE JUST THE STEM END of each tomato. Slice all the tomatoes and set aside. Slice all the mozzarella and set aside. The salad can be assembled individually on plates by stacking some of each type of tomato with slices of cheese and basil, or it can be assembled on a platter. The

cherry tomatoes can be scattered about or threaded onto a bamboo skewer for effect.

DRIZZLE THE DRESSING over the tomatoes and garnish with a few grinds of pepper.

Serves 6

Spring Herb Salad, Grilled Lamb, Feta Eggplant Baba Ghanoush

One of my pals claims we are genetically wired to love the flavor of charred lamb fat, and those who don't have tried to alter their authentic selves. This babble comes from someone who eats way too much animal fat and has squandered a fortune on Côtes du Rhône, not an easy thing to do. Nonetheless, there is something primal about grilling, probably why men like it so much. Not that women don't like primal things too, we just veer in a different direction. All the little herbs, for instance. I feel totally in touch with my primal self in the garden, snipping the ends off all the little herbs.

For the Baba Ghanoush

1 eggplant
Salt
Olive oil for drizzling
2 anchovies
4 cloves garlic
Juice and grated zest of 1 lemon
Freshly ground black pepper
½ cup crumbled feta cheese

PEEL AND SLICE THE EGGPLANT into ½-inch slices, place on paper towels, and sprinkle with salt. Let the eggplant sit at room temperature for 1 hour. Then wipe the eggplant dry and place on an oiled sheet pan.

PREHEAT THE OVEN TO 400°F. Drizzle the eggplant slices with olive oil and a little more salt. Roast for 10 minutes or so, until the eggplant is soft to the touch. Remove from the oven and let cool.

IN A LARGE BOWL, mash together the eggplant, anchovies, garlic, lemon juice and zest, and pepper. Add the feta. Set aside.

For the Lamb

1½ teaspoons dried oregano
2 pounds lamb shoulder, cut into largish (1½ inches or so) chunks
Salt and freshly ground black pepper

LIGHT A FIRE IN A CHARCOAL GRILL, or preheat a gas grill. Soak eight 6-inch bamboo skewers in water for at least a half hour to prevent them from burning, or use metal skewers. Crumble the oregano between your palms to release the flavor, and dust the chunks of lamb well, then salt and pepper them and thread them onto the skewers. Grill over a medium fire for about 2 minutes per side for medium rare.

To Assemble

4 cups spring garden greens, such as mizuna, sorrel, arugula, parsley, watercress, bergamot, and/or mint

PLACE A CUP OF GREENS on each plate and top with the hot lamb. The heat of the lamb will wilt the greens, and the juices stand in for a dressing. Top the lamb chunks with a dollop of the baba ghanoush and serve.

Serves 6 as an appetizer or 4 as a main course

Grilled Asparagus, Bresaola, Shaved Parmesan

Bresaola is a tenderloin of beef cured Italian-style, like prosciutto. We serve it in the spring when the first of our Washington asparagus arrives. There have been one-day trips over the Cascades to Prosser: we visit Kay Simon at her Chinook Winery and grab some cases of vino, and then head down the road for as much "fat grass" as we can find. Those pencil-thin stalks of asparagus are for the birds.

For the Asparagus

> *36 fat spears of asparagus (6 per person), washed and trimmed*
> *Olive oil for drizzling*
> *Coarse salt*

BRING YOUR GRILL (or sauté pan) to a good sizzle. In a large, flat pan, place the trimmed asparagus in a row, heads lined up. This will make it easier to move the stalks around for cooking and serving. Drizzle the oil over the stalks and roll them gently to moisten them completely. Too much oil will cause your grill to smoke and leave black soot on the asparagus. Sprinkle with coarse salt and set aside while you make the vinaigrette.

For the Vinaigrette

> *1 cup really good olive oil (here's where you want to use that expensive*
> *extra virgin oil)*
> *⅓ cup fresh lemon juice*
> *Grated zest of 1 lemon*
> *Grated zest of 1 orange*
> *1 teaspoon freshly ground black pepper*
> *1 tablespoon chopped fresh lemon mint, or verbena, or other garden mint*

IN A SMALL BOWL, whisk together the olive oil and lemon juice. Add the remaining ingredients, whisk, and reserve.

To Assemble

18 paper-thin slices bresaola (3 per person)
8 ounces Parmesan cheese, in a chunk

USING TONGS, place the asparagus on the grill, and grill for about 2 minutes per side. Put the asparagus on a platter and dress with the slices of bresaola. Using a peeler, shave slivers of Parmesan over the bresaola, and drizzle with vinaigrette. Serve immediately.

Serves 6

Asparagus

WHEN YOU DRIVE EAST FROM SEATTLE OVER THE CASCADE MOUNTAINS, the landscape changes after the pass at Snoqualamie. In a few miles, the conifer forests of the mythical Northwest, a result of the languid days of rain, give way to the vast grasslands of the eastern slope. As you descend further toward the valley of the mighty Columbia and its tributaries, the Yakima and Snake Rivers, the scattered pines grow sparser until the irrigated farmlands spread out in a jumble of orchards, vineyards, and hayfields. Somewhere in this once rich, dry soil, the moist sandy loam provides fertile ground for *Asparagus officinalis,* once popularly known as sparrowgrass. ASPARAGUS, OR "GRASS" AS IT IS KNOWN IN THE TRADE, is the true harbinger of spring in the Pacific Northwest. I have set for myself a seasonal culinary calendar: like all those who cook professionally and in large quantities with no boundaries or bosses to answer to, it was necessary to provide some structure for my work. Since the food revolution and the wonders of air freight now provide us with produce from all seasons and climes around the world, in some places twenty-four hours a day, it is even more important now than in the past to draw the line somewhere. For me, that meant first making a circle around my small green island, and second around my true homeland, the State of Washington. This ordered my work life, gave parameters to my creativity, provided discipline, and gave me a living relationship with the seasons. By the end of February I have been roasting parsnips, peeling beets, making sweet potato fritters, and braising beans and short ribs since before Thanksgiving, so I am truly excited to see the first little heads of asparagus pushing their way up through the bleak garden landscape. Green! Asparagus is an ancient grass, touted for its heft by Pliny and used as a cure by medieval *curanderos*. It grows easily and well in sandy, drained soil, and even though the planted crowns may take three years to produce a spear, after the first crop the hardy roots can produce and prosper for decades. ❑ ASPARAGUS AFICIONADOS ARE QUITE SPECIFIC about the way asparagus should be cooked. Actually, that is not true. What we are all specific about are the results. Cook it any way you want; just make sure it is bright green, firm but tender, intact but not sandy. The common fallacy is that pencil-thin asparagus is somehow the best. Nonsense: the thicker the better. Remember that asparagus is a stem, and stems are conduits of moisture to the flower. A thin stem is fibrous, almost all tubes to take up moisture. A piece of "fat grass" has the same tubes, but lots of space between them filled with thick luscious flesh, and thus is more flavorful, more tender. A half-pound asparagus stalk is a scintillating piece of wonder. ❑ SELECT THE THICKEST STEMS YOU CAN FIND, and look for heads that are tight and smooth. If the tops are feathery, they have got some age. I tend to trim the stalks by 4 to 6 inches, depending on size. The old saw about breaking the stalks where they are tender can waste a lot of good asparagus. I cut them on the diagonal with a knife. The little folded-up leaves along the stalk can harbor dirt or sand. The only surefire way to remove it is to peel the stalks gently, starting a little below the head. Once the stalks are peeled, they should be cooked soon; otherwise they dry out. You can also soak them in cold water and gently scrub the stems with a soft brush to remove the dirt. ▪▪▪ COOK IT QUICK—a minute in boiling water or a few minutes on the grill. Spears of different thicknesses will cook differently, so keep an eye on them. The vivid green spears need little in the way of adornment. A little butter, or lemon, or sea salt, or really good olive oil—my favorite—is all it takes for asparagus to give us its glory. Heap it on.

Classic Duck Salad

Here's another classic salad from the restaurant's early days. The first time I tasted it, it was made by my new pantry guy with leftover duck necks and wings. Then I saw Wolfgang Puck make it on TV. Next, it was all over restaurant menus, including mine! This salad was so good and so popular that we couldn't get enough duck trim to meet the demand, so we had to start buying whole ducks. Naturally, we had to raise the price to cover the cost. And of course the high price reduced the demand until finally everybody was tired of duck salad and we all moved on to something else.

For the Dressing

⅓ cup raspberry vinegar
⅔ cup walnut oil
Salt and freshly ground black pepper to taste

IN A MEDIUM BOWL, whisk all ingredients together until the oil and vinegar emulsify.

To Assemble

12 ounces slivered, cooked duck meat
½ cup thinly sliced red onion
¼ cup pine nuts
¼ cup julienned parsnip
6 cups loosely packed Bibb lettuce leaves

IN A LARGE METAL BOWL, toss the duck with the onion, nuts, and parsnips. Add ½ cup of the dressing, toss, and place the bowl in a 350°F oven for 5 minutes, or until the dressing just begins to sizzle. Remove from the oven and toss with the greens while still hot. Serve immediately.

Serves 4

My Granny's Winter Salad

I suspect lots of grannies made this salad in the days before corporate agriculture started providing us with year-round fruits and vegetables. As recently as the 1950s, the produce aisle at the supermarket had a completely different look at different times of the year. During the winter it was pretty bleak. For my grandmother, who lived thirty miles from the nearest grocery store, it was especially so. At the ranch, this salad was made with the little mandarin oranges that always showed up in the stores around the holidays. Wrapped in blue tissue and nestled inside little wooden crates labeled with exotic calligraphy, the oranges were a magical treat in the dark and cold days of winter.

For the Dressing

½ cup cider vinegar
1½ cups nonassertive olive oil
2 tablespoons honey, or more to taste
1 teaspoon freshly ground black pepper
1 tablespoon chopped flat-leaf parsley
Salt

IN A MEDIUM BOWL, whisk all the ingredients together and taste. Since honeys have different degrees of sweetness, you may want to add more.

To Assemble

1 grapefruit
2 mandarin oranges
1 small red onion, peeled
2 avocados

SECTION THE GRAPEFRUIT and the mandarin orange, being careful to remove all the pith. Slice the onion very thin and then cut it into ¼-inch pieces. Peel and slice the avocados. Combine the citrus, avocado, and enough dressing to moisten all ingredients. Toss gently and serve immediately.

Serves 4

Greens

IT WAS ONLY A FEW YEARS AGO THAT THE PRODUCE SECTION OF YOUR average grocery offered just a few types of lettuce: iceberg, romaine, green leaf, Bibb in the winter, and sometimes spinach. That was it. Remarkably, a stroll through the produce aisles now might require a guidebook if one wanted the names and origins of the myriad greens, globes, bunches, and tangles of the wild and exotic foods to be found there. Look no farther than your local grocery for the truest statement of American diversity. If one cooks for a living, all this makes for fascinating times in the kitchen. ■ AN ADVENTUROUS STREAK IS A GOOD THING in the kitchen. It doesn't apply just to eating; it involves the shopping as well. Find something unknown that looks interesting, take it home, and try to figure out what to do with it. My mother the gardener liked to play "stump the chef." I would find a box of strange purple orbs covered with dirt clods at the kitchen door. An hour later, the phone would ring: "Did you find the kohlrabi?" The fact that it had taken six months to nurture these to harvest (not to mention the compost) was not lost on me. Neither was the fact that not once had she ever mentioned that she was growing this peculiar vegetable. ■ I LEARNED A GREAT DEAL from the indexes of old cookbooks. It turns out there is nothing really new at all. In fact, what is new was once old, and what is old sometimes turns out to be very new. Arugula is a good example. Known as "rocket" to the settlers who brought it with them to the West, and still called rocket in England, arugula has been on a trend arc in the foodie subcult for several years now. It is touted as an Italian green on fancy menus but grows on roadsides all over if you look. It self-sows in the garden and will grow all winter if there's no hard freeze. I love the stuff. It has a nutty, aromatic flavor and, depending on the age of the leaf, it can get quite hot. Flea beetles love it too, and the best organic rocket has tiny holes all over the leaves. ⏲ ICEBERG LETTUCE FELL INTO DISFAVOR with my set about thirty years ago. Flavorless, bland, and wet, it was the original engineered corporate food. Grown quickly for mass consumption, it was the white bread of the produce aisle, the epitome of ordinary. A seventy-day crop, iceberg could make or break a Salinas Valley farmer twice in one year. Boxcars stacked to the ceiling with cases of it moved out across the country like lava. I love the stuff. Give me a tuna sandwich with big chunks of iceberg any day. Water flies when you bite into iceberg, and there is nothing like it for crisp and crunch. Sure enough, iceberg lettuce is staging a comeback. The trendiest restaurants are sporting iceberg wedge salads on their menus. *Food Arts* magazine recently featured a recipe for an iceberg salad! What could be more enticing to a generation raised on bitter, tight-flavored, and sometimes tough radicchio than the bright, light, flavorless flavor of the once lowly iceberg?

Poached Salmon, Lemon Ginger Aïoli

In the heat of a summer evening, a cool, crisp salad with gently cooked fish makes a breezy, elegant little meal. You can cook the fish ahead and chill it or cook it just before serving, letting it cool for a few moments. The poached fish is very fragile when it is still warm. You could add some cherry tomatoes or olives to this salad. For me, the appeal of this salad is its stark simplicity, and the delicate, moist salmon.

For the Poached Salmon

2 cups white wine
½ onion, thinly sliced
1 bay leaf
6 peppercorns
6 whole cloves
1 lemon, thinly sliced
4 salmon fillets, 3 to 5 ounces each, skin on

PREHEAT THE OVEN TO 350°F. In a large, deep roasting pan, combine the wine, onion, bay leaf, peppercorns, cloves, and lemon slices. Place the salmon fillets in the pan, skin side down, and fill with water until the fillets are covered. Place the pan in the oven for 15 minutes, or until the fillets feel firm to the touch. Remove from the oven and let the salmon cool in the poaching liquid. After they have cooled enough to touch, carefully peel the skin off the salmon and discard. Carefully remove the fillets to a platter for chilling, if desired.

For the Aïoli

FOLLOW THE RECIPE for Homemade Mayonnaise on page 8, substituting rice wine vinegar for the lemon juice. Before you add the oil, add 2 tablespoons Pickled Ginger (see page 17), 2 tablespoons white miso, and the grated zest of 1 lemon. Process until puréed, and then add the oil as directed for the mayonnaise.

To Assemble

4 cups mixed greens
Lemon wedges for garnish

TO SERVE, place a piece of the poached salmon on a cup or so of the greens. Garnish with a generous spoonful of the aïoli and a lemon wedge.

Serves 4

Chef's Tip: The poaching liquid can be saved and used as fish stock. Chill the stock. The detritus should settle on the bottom. Carefully pour off the top two-thirds of the liquid and reserve. Discard the remainder.

Fennel, Parmesan, Zested Lemon Vinaigrette

We drove from Venice to Genoa at breakneck speed. We had portobello panini at a gas station on the auto route (delicious) that I bought while my husband, Bruce, was fueling the Lancia. We got back in the car and proceeded to have a big fight—about what? I can't remember. We made up just as we saw the road signs for Reggio. I remember nothing of the town except the big stone arch where we parked the car. We were the only people who sat outside in the waning fall sun. Paper napkins and tin tables, but the salad was something to remember.

The fennel bulbs for this salad must be cut very thin or they are too tough to eat without cooking. We use a mandoline at the restaurant. I haven't specified a type of greens for this recipe because I like to take advantage of the freshest ones available. This salad is best, however, with a single green, rather than the sometimes raggedy "gourmet mixed greens." I like mizuna, arugula, or Lolla Rossa.

For the Vinaigrette

Juice and grated zest of 1 lemon
1 teaspoon honey
1 teaspoon sugar
½ to 1 cup good-quality olive oil, depending on the tartness of the lemon
Freshly ground black pepper (optional)

WHISK THE DRESSING ingredients together until emulsified.

To Assemble

8 cups of a single green, such as mizuna, arugula, or Lolla Rossa
1 fennel bulb, very thinly sliced
4 ounces Parmigiano-Reggiano cheese

ASSEMBLE THE SALAD ingredients on a plate, starting with the greens on the bottom. Scatter the thin fennel slices over the top, and use a peeler to shave the cheese over all. Drizzle with a little of the dressing.

Serves 6 to 8

Grilled Ahi Niçoise, Pea Shoots, Wrinkled Olive Tapenade

In the trade we call this a composed salad. This is because it is made up of varied ingredients that are composed on the plate rather than being tossed together. The *salade niçoise* is a French classic that originated in the Mediterranean town of Nice. Much of the famous "cuisine of the sun" originated there—*à la niçoise* is a familiar phrase for us foodies. When I make this salad and imagine the flavor, I always think of my mother and the funny little *tabac* on the rue Cambon where we ate salads after being up all night and drank wine and listened to the pinball games chortle and bang. Don't let the ingredient list scare you off. Most of the vegetables can be prepared in advance, so it becomes a great one-dish meal for a luncheon or a casual summer get-together. Julia Child has railed against making this with fresh tuna. She prefers the canned. I prefer the fresh. You can easily have it either way.

For the Olive Tapenade

¾ cup pitted olives, niçoise style or oil cured
2 tablespoons fresh parsley
1 teaspoon fresh lemon juice
3 anchovies
3 cloves garlic
1 tablespoon extra virgin olive oil
Freshly ground black pepper (optional)

PLACE ALL THE INGREDIENTS in a food processor and pulse until finely chopped.

To Assemble

6 tuna fillets, 4 ounces each
Olive oil for rubbing onto tuna
6 cups fresh pea shoots or other crunchy greens

8 ounces baby French green beans, blanched and chilled
8 ounces tiny red potatoes, cooked and chilled
1 pint cherry tomatoes
½ pint niçoise-style olives
Lemon juice for drizzling
Freshly ground black pepper
Lemon wedges for garnish

LIGHT A FIRE in a charcoal grill, or preheat a gas grill. Rub both sides of the tuna fillets with olive oil and grill over medium coals for 3 minutes per side. Arrange the pea shoots, green beans, potatoes, tomatoes, and olives on a platter or individual plates in a manner that pleases your eye. Drizzle with the lemon juice and a few cranks of black pepper if you like. Place the grilled fillets alongside, and garnish with a spoonful of the tapenade and fresh lemon wedges.

Serves 6

Soups

Garden Tomato Soup, Tomato Basil Pistou

Wild Mushroom Soup, Parmesan Toast

Fireside Oyster Stew

Roasted Garlic Soup

Six Lilies Soup

Crab Bisque, Crab Fritters

Curried Summer Squash Soup

Rocket Soup, Chèvre Rye Toast

Cold Halibut Ceviche Soup, Cucumber Salsa

Lovage Soup, Shrimp Toast

Smoky Potato Soup, Salmon Caviar

Hot and Sour Fish Soup

Mussel and Clam Chowder

Cauliflower Soup

Garden Tomato Soup, Tomato Basil Pistou, page 100; Curried Summer Squash Soup, page 114

Garden Tomato Soup, Tomato Basil Pistou

The soul of this recipe comes from my friend, the aforementioned Tomato Queen. I naturally have made a few changes, one of which involves using a tomato press. If you are a tomato lover, gardener, canning maven, or even just a fussy eater, this is the kitchen toy for you. You clamp the contraption to the counter, drop halved tomatoes in the big funnel on top, turn the crank, and watch as the sieve at the bottom oozes beautiful tomato pulp: no skins, no seeds, just quarts of pure tomato bliss.

This soup is a showstopper for garden-ripe tomatoes, and it can be served warm or chilled. Don't heat it more than once, though, or the flavor will change drastically.

For the Pistou

2 large, ripe tomatoes, peeled, seeded (see Chef's Tip below), and cut in ¼- to ½-inch dice
1 cup basil leaves, chopped
4 cloves garlic, very finely minced
2 tablespoons chopped parsley
Salt

BLEND ALL THE INGREDIENTS TOGETHER in a bowl and let the flavors marry for 1 hour or so before serving.

For the Soup

8 to 10 large, garden-ripe tomatoes
⅓ to ½ cup good sherry vinegar
Salt
About 1 tablespoon sugar

CUT THE TOMATOES INTO QUARTERS and process them through a tomato press, or peel, seed, and chop the tomatoes by hand, taking care to preserve all the juice. A high-quality juicer that preserves the pulp can also be used. Heat the tomato purée in a pot, and taste it to determine the amount of sweet and tart needed to amplify the fresh tomato flavor. Season with the vinegar, salt, and sugar accordingly. For the chilled version, follow the same steps once the soup is cold. Serve either really hot or really cold, with a heaping tablespoon of pistou in the bowl.

Makes 8 generous servings

Chef's Tip: To peel and seed tomatoes drop whole tomatoes into boiling water. Boil for 1 minute. Drain the tomatoes and chill. Skins will slide off easily after being pricked with a paring knife.

To seed tomatoes, cut in half, leaving the stem at one end. Scoop out the seeds from the pockets at each end with your fingers.

Wild Mushroom Soup, Parmesan Toast

The San Juan Islands are a great place for "'shrooming." In the fall and spring, boxes appear at the back door, brought by Toussaint or the guy we know only as "'shroom man." We joke that his eyes are pinwheels, and once, when I asked him to whom I should make the check, he replied, "Me." Picking mushrooms randomly can be dangerous, so I buy only those that I know. Boletes, chanterelles, princes, morels, and even porcini have been found in the islands. Years ago, a friend planted several acres of hazelnut trees injected with truffle spores. We had high hopes, but, alas, the truffle crop seems to have failed. I wouldn't dream of mixing true wild mushrooms in this soup. Each mushroom has a distinct and unique flavor, not meant to be confused in combination. So use any one of the mushroom varieties mentioned.

1 tablespoon finely chopped garlic
1 medium onion, finely chopped
1½ pounds chanterelle, hedgehog, morel, bolete, or other mushrooms
2 tablespoons unsalted butter
1 teaspoon whole dried marjoram leaves
2 cups chicken stock
2 cups beef stock
2 cups heavy cream or half-and-half
1 heaping tablespoon Dijon mustard
Salt and freshly ground black pepper
Chopped chives for garnish

IN A LARGE POT, sweat the garlic, onions, and mushrooms in the butter by keeping the heat on low, placing a piece of parchment or wax paper directly on top of the ingredients, and covering the pot tightly, for at least 30 minutes. This step allows the ingredients to release their moisture and flavor while cooking without their liquids evaporating. When the mixture is softened and aromatic, add the marjoram and stocks, turn up the heat a little, and simmer gently for 20 minutes or so. Then, in a blender or food processor, purée the mixture until smooth. Return it to the pot, raise the heat, and add the cream and mustard, and salt and pepper to taste.

SERVE IMMEDIATELY WHILE HOT. Garnish the bowls with fresh chives.

Note: This soup will keep in the refrigerator for 3 days. You can freeze the puréed mushroom mixture for 6 weeks. Use caution when reheating the soup once you've added the cream, because it could scorch.

Serves 6 to 8

For the Parmesan Toasts

6 thin slices baguette or other crusty bread like como or ciabatta
Olive oil for brushing
½ cup grated Parmigiano-Reggiano cheese

BRUSH BOTH SIDES OF THE BAGUETTE slices with olive oil. Place the bread on a sheet pan and sprinkle each slice with a generous amount of the cheese. Toast in a 450°F oven for 10 minutes, or until the tops are golden and crispy.

Chef's Tip: Don't be discouraged if you can't go mushroom hunting yourself. Just use cremini or button mushrooms from the grocery instead!

Soup

THERE ARE DAYS WHEN NOTHING BUT SOUP WILL DO. DAYS WHEN THE duties are too many, the pace is too fast, and a recent round of dinner parties, fancy lunches, and restaurant meals has left me feeling that life has been a little too racy and wild. Soup is a culinary cure-all. Even if it's not easy to eat in bed, it is the classic restorative for any and all ailments. Chicken soup, puréed soup (no chewing necessary), even milk heated with medicinal herbs is a time-honored soother for the invalid or for those just feeling woozy. Winter nights at home are perfect for a steaming bowl and a slice of crusty bread. ▣ PUTTERING AROUND THE KITCHEN is a favorite way to spend my winter afternoons, ignoring the darkening sky and doing something productive. Combining pantry organizing and soup making is as good a way as any to do this. If I start with the refrigerator, I may find something to inspire my soup efforts, like a small chunk of ham or some odds and ends of cheeses. ▣ THE FIRST THING TO DO is decide how you want the soup to taste—not specifically, but more stylistically. Clear and bright (chicken stock, ginger, cilantro, green vegetables like peapods, bok choy, or broccoli)? Hot and zesty (chorizo, beef or ham stock, tomatoes, chiles)? Rich and dark (lentils, chicken stock, ham, garlic)? Rich and light (milk, potatoes, onions, shrimp)? ❚❚❘❚❚ STOCK IS THE BACKBONE OF A WELL-FLAVORED SOUP. You can make your own, or you can buy it. Don't let not having the time or energy for making stock stop you from making soup. Store-bought stock can be almost as good as homemade. Soup does not have to cook for hours and hours either. That myth sometimes produces nothing but a bowl of gooey sludge. ❚❚❘❚❚ SOUP MAKING IS USUALLY an exercise in restraint. It is tempting to just start throwing stuff in. But as your enthusiasm for the project builds, so does the tendency toward excess. Too many ingredients can muddy the flavors, cause textures to be lost, and diminish a soup's distinction and personality. ❚❚❘❚❚ MANY COOKS WANT TO GET heavy-handed with the pepper. Dumping in the black pepper or, worse, the red pepper flakes is usually a last-ditch attempt to make it taste like something. Do not succumb to this temptation. Moderation is all. People can add salt and pepper on their own later. ❚❚❘❚❚ ALL FOODS HAVE THEIR NATURAL PARTNERS. Discovering the partner of your favorite ingredient is the adventure of making soup.

Fireside Oyster Stew

In my family, oyster stew on Christmas Eve is a tradition. Stew is a misnomer because this soup requires only a few minutes on the stove; anything more and the oysters become lumpy and tough. I have had fun substituting different types of alcohol: single-malt scotch adds that peaty, dark bass note; brandy, an earthy finish; sherry, the classic cream soup jolt; Wild Turkey, a vague sweetness. This is what's fun about cooking—the endless variations on a theme. You can make this stew ahead by leaving out the oysters and fresh herbs. Reheat it gently and add the oysters and herbs to poach for a few minutes just before serving.

> ¼ cup (½ stick) unsalted butter
> 4 shallots, finely minced
> ¼ cup brandy
> 4 cups heavy cream
> 2 ounces pale dry sherry
> 16 yearling or small oysters, shucked (see page 64), with the liquor
>   reserved
> ½ cup chopped flat-leaf Italian parsley
> 1 tablespoon chopped fresh thyme
> Salt and freshly ground black pepper
> ¼ cup (½ stick) unsalted butter, clarified (see Chef's Tip below)

IN A LARGE POT, melt the butter over medium heat and sauté the shallots until they are translucent. Add the brandy and stir to deglaze the pan, igniting it to burn off the alcohol. Add the cream and sherry and heat to bubbling. Reduce the cream for a few minutes to thicken it, then add the oysters and poach for 2 minutes, over medium heat, or until the edges of each oyster just begin to curl and the oyster firms up.

REMOVE FROM THE HEAT and fold in the parsley and thyme. Add salt and pepper to taste. Serve in warmed bowls and drizzle a little of the clarified butter on top for garnish.

Serves 4

Chef's Tip: To clarify butter melt the butter in the microwave for a minute or over low on the stove. The butter will separate. The oil will float on the top and the whey solids will sink to the bottom. Clarified butter will take a lot more heat without burning than melted butter.

Roasted Garlic Soup

This is a soup for fall. When the days get short and the wind blows, we cannot make enough of it at the restaurant. I adapted a clever method for peeling garlic. My mother always peeled shallots by dropping them in boiling water for a minute or so, so I started doing the same thing with the pounds of garlic needed in the kitchen. We reduced garlic-prepping time by an hour. I was astonished the first time I saw peeled garlic in three-pound jars in a store, but was disappointed to discover the pale flavor. Preparing the garlic yourself makes all the difference.

4 heads garlic
1 tablespoon water
2 yellow onions, peeled and chopped
3 cups chicken stock
2 russet potatoes, cooked and peeled
2 fresh pasilla or Anaheim chiles
1 cup heavy cream
1 cup buttermilk
1 cup grated mild cheddar cheese
½ cup chopped chives

PREHEAT THE OVEN TO 300°F. Trim all the extra paperlike skin from the garlic bulbs. Place the bulbs in a pie pan with the water, and cover with foil. Roast in the oven for 45 minutes.

MEANWHILE, IN A LARGE SAUCEPAN, combine the onions and chicken stock, bring to a boil, and cook for 35 minutes, until the onions are soft and translucent. Cut the cooked potatoes into large pieces and add them to the stock. Lower the heat and simmer for 30 minutes or so.

TO ROAST THE PASILLAS, preheat the oven to 450°F. Place the peppers on a sheet pan and roast for 15 minutes. Remove and let cool. Remove the skins; they should peel off easily. Carefully remove the seeds, chop the pasillas into ¼-inch dice, and reserve.

AFTER THE ROASTED GARLIC HAS COOLED, hold the root end of the bulb and gently squeeze the cooked pulp into the stock mixture. Purée the mixture in a food processor or blender and return to the pan. Add the cream and buttermilk and heat gently, adding the grated cheese as you go. When the soup is hot, fold in the roasted chiles. Serve in warmed bowls with chopped chives for garnish.

Serves 8 generously

Six Lilies Soup

H⟨⟨⟨⟨⟩⟩⟩H

I distinctly remember making this soup for the first time in the fall of 1981. In the early years of the restaurant, my mother's garden provided almost all of our produce. We just took what she sent us and figured out our menu around what we found in the boxes. My mother had little understanding of restaurants or how they worked, but she was an excellent cook and a botanist. One box she sent contained two onions, four leeks, a handful of shallots, two heads of garlic, a bundle of chives, and some green onions that, frankly, were way past their prime. I called her. "What's with the onions and stuff? That isn't enough to do anything with." She chuckled and queried, "Don't you know what those are? Those are the six lilies, Liliaceae, all members of the same family." I was exasperated because I had only about an hour before I needed at least fifty servings of some kind of soup. "What to do?" I moaned into the phone. "Make a soup," she said and hung up. And so a soup was born. The amounts of the various lilies are flexible. You can also leave out the cream altogether and replace it with additional stock.

1 large onion, coarsely chopped
1 large leek, coarsely chopped
6 shallots, coarsely chopped
4 to 6 cloves garlic, flattened with a knife
6 green onions, coarsely chopped
¼ cup (½ stick) unsalted butter
3 cups chicken stock
3 cups beef stock
1 cup half-and-half
Sherry to taste (pale dry preferred)
½ cup chopped chives

IN A LARGE POT, sweat the onion, leek, shallots, garlic, and green onions in the butter by keeping the heat on low, placing a piece of parchment or wax paper directly on top of the ingredients, and covering the pot tightly, for 20 minutes, or until soft. This step allows the ingredients to release their moisture and flavor while cooking without their liquids evaporating. Add the stocks and continue to cook for 10 minutes. Remove from the heat, add the half-and-half and sherry to taste, and purée in a food processor or blender. Heat gently, and serve garnished with the chives.

Serves 8 as a first course

Crab Bisque, Crab Fritters

The Dungeness crab *(Cancer magister)* should be Washington's state crustacean. It thrives in the shallow coves and bays of our region. When we were kids, my grandfather would take us out on the log booms at low tide with rakes and buckets. We would snag the crabs as they scuttled sideways to find shade under the floating logs. It was years before I realized how dangerous this activity was for children, but I felt safe following Grampa as he leapt from log to log with the rake in one hand and a bucket of crabs in the other.

Bisque is a smooth soup. This one gets its depth of flavor from the crab shells. The crunch of the fritter is a tasty foil for the soup's silken texture.

For the Crab Bisque

>2 large Dungeness crabs, cooked
>1 red onion
>4 stalks celery, coarsely chopped
>8½ cups water
>1 tablespoon plus ½ teaspoon salt
>1 cup heavy cream
>½ cup chopped fresh tarragon
>½ cup Pernod
>2 tablespoons cornstarch
>White pepper

CLEAN THE MEAT FROM THE CRABS and reserve it for the bisque and the fritters. Preheat the oven to 350°F. Place the crab shells in a sheet pan with half the onion, cut into wedges, and half the celery, and roast for 30 minutes. In a large stockpot, combine the roasted crab shells, onion, and celery with 8 cups of the water. Bring to a boil and simmer for 40 minutes. Strain off the shells and scraps. Reduce the crab stock until you have 4 cups left.

CHOP THE REMAINING ONION AND CELERY and add to the crab stock with 1 tablespoon salt. Cook over high heat for 20 minutes. Add a third of the crabmeat and continue to cook for another 10 minutes. Purée in a food processor or blender until completely smooth, then strain through a China cap or other fine-mesh strainer. Return the strained soup to the pot over medium-high heat and add the cream, tarragon, and Pernod. In a small bowl, whisk together the remaining ½ cup water and cornstarch until smooth. Whisk into the soup and stir until the soup thickens. Add the remaining ½ teaspoon salt and white pepper to taste. Serve hot in warm bowls with a crab fritter (recipe follows) on top.

For the Crab Fritters

Two-thirds of the crabmeat from the original 2 crabs
1 egg
1 tablespoon bread crumbs, plus about 1 cup more for dredging
1 tablespoon finely chopped onion
1 tablespoon finely chopped red bell pepper
2 tablespoons mayonnaise
1 cup peanut oil for frying (optional)

IN A MEDIUM BOWL, mix together the crabmeat, egg, 1 tablespoon bread crumbs, onion, bell pepper, and mayonnaise. Form into 6 patties. Place about 1 cup bread crumbs in a shallow plate, and dredge the patties in the crumbs. Chill for 1 hour. You can bake or fry the fritters To fry them, heat the peanut oil to 350°F in a small deep saucepan, add the fritters, and fry for 6 minutes, or until golden. Or, to bake them, preheat the oven to 400°F, place the fritters on a baking sheet, and bake for 10 minutes, or until golden.

Serves 6

Curried Summer Squash Soup

This is one of the most requested recipes from my kitchen. The secret ingredient is buttermilk. Stuck with several quarts of the stuff following a typical order mixup, and short of the cream I thought I needed, I discovered the power of adventuring with food. This soup can be made with zucchini, but I prefer the bright yellow squash of summer. Try serving it cold on a hot summer night.

All curry powders are different, sometimes significantly so. Curry heat can be mild or very hot, so use this spice blend to your own taste.

6 summer squash, ends trimmed, cut into 1-inch chunks
1 onion, chopped
6 cloves garlic, crushed
¼ cup (½ stick) unsalted butter
1 to 4 tablespoons curry powder
3 cups chicken stock
2 tablespoons arrowroot
4 cups buttermilk
1 red bell pepper, roasted (see Chef's Tip), peeled, and seeded
½ cup chopped cilantro

IN A DEEP POT with a tight-fitting lid, sweat the squash, onion, and garlic in the butter and curry powder by keeping the heat on low, placing a piece of parchment or wax paper directly on top of the ingredients, and covering the pot tightly for 1 hour. This step allows the ingredients to release their moisture and flavor while cooking without their liquids evaporating. Add 1 cup of the stock, raise the heat to high, and cook for 10 minutes. Purée the mixture in a food processor or blender until smooth. Add the arrowroot and purée again. Heat the mixture with the remaining 2 cups stock, and add the buttermilk.

PURÉE THE RED PEPPER in a food processor or blender until smooth.

DRIZZLE SOME OF THE PURÉE on each bowl of soup, and garnish with the cilantro.

Serves 6

Chef's Tip: For roasted peppers, heat the oven to 400°F and place sweet red bell peppers on a sheet pan. Roast for 15 to 20 minutes, or until the skin colors and starts to wrinkle. This works well with yellow peppers too. For some reason this doesn't work with green peppers, probably because they are not as ripe. Let the peppers cool for about 30 minutes. Then slide the skins off, tear in half, and carefully remove all of the seeds. This will be easier if you run the peppers under water, but you will also lose some of the flavor.

Rocket Soup, Chèvre Rye Toast

Rocket, or arugula as it is known in the Italian culinary world, is a cool-weather green that grows best in the fall and spring. It is also what gardeners call "invasive," in that it spreads itself around everywhere. That's fine with me. I like the strong, peppery flavor and find it useful in many ways. This soup is the direct result of having lots and lots of it, more than we could ever use in salads. Rocket loses some of its bite in the soup but manages to keep its distinctive nutty flavor.

At the restaurant, we have a lot of fun coming up with simple accompaniments for the different soups we serve, and the chèvre rye toast is a favorite. Really good chèvre is the key. In the Pacific Northwest, we have several intrepid cheese makers, and, indeed, it takes real devotion to make good cheese. The livestock alone is a major commitment: when they need milking, you must be there. I like the soft chèvre from Rolling Stone in Idaho for this toast. I like to think the goats would be proud of their contribution.

2 leeks, white part only
10 cloves garlic
3 tablespoons olive oil
2 cups chicken stock
8 to 10 cups arugula
2 cups heavy cream
Salt and freshly ground black pepper

CHOP THE LEEKS INTO 1-INCH PIECES and crush the garlic. Place the leeks and garlic in a large pot with the oil, place a piece of parchment or wax paper directly on top of the ingredients, cover the pot tightly, and sweat over low heat for 15 minutes or so, then add the stock and rocket. Cook for another 10 minutes or so, then purée the soup in a food processor or blender. Return the mixture to the pot and whisk in

the cream while heating. Add salt and pepper to taste. Serve hot, garnished with the chèvre rye toast (recipe follows).

Serves 4 to 6

For the Toast

> *4 slices soft chèvre or goat cheese*
> *4 slices dark rye bread*
> *Olive oil for brushing*

PREHEAT THE BROILER. Spread the chèvre on the bread, cut the slices
into quarters, brush with oil, and broil for a few minutes, until the
bread is crispy at the edges and the cheese is soft. Pass the extra toast
at the table.

Makes 16 toasts

Cold Halibut Ceviche Soup, Cucumber Salsa

This is a cold soup meant to be served when the weather is warm, the tomatoes are ripe from the garden, and the halibut is opalescent and tender, just up from deep in the Sound. These perfect ingredients create a simple summer soup so alive with the soul of island life that I beam with pleasure when I make it, look at it, and taste it. I take a provincial joy in seeing my customers get what is great about Northwest—here in a backwater, upstairs over a gas station—cuisine.

½ cup lime juice
¼ cup rice wine vinegar
8 to 12 ounces halibut, cut into ¼-inch chunks
½ medium red onion, slivered
1 tablespoon chopped garlic
Crushed dried red chiles (optional)
½ red bell pepper, cut into ⅛-inch dice
4 cups tomato juice or fresh tomato purée (see Garden Tomato Soup,
*   page 100)*
Salt and freshly ground black pepper

IN A LARGE, NONREACTIVE CONTAINER, drizzle the lime juice and vinegar over the halibut chunks. Toss together with the onion, garlic, and crushed red chiles, and refrigerate overnight. Before serving, mix the halibut with the bell pepper and tomato juice. Salt and pepper to taste. Chill and serve in cold bowls with a generous spoonful of cucumber salsa (recipe follows) on top.

Serves 4 to 6

For the Salsa

> 1 large cucumber, peeled, seeded, and cut into ⅛-inch dice
> 2 tablespoons finely chopped cilantro
> 1 tablespoon finely chopped Pickled Ginger (page 17)
> 2 tablespoons seasoned rice wine vinegar

MIX ALL INGREDIENTS TOGETHER in a small bowl. Store in the refrigerator until ready to use. The salsa keeps for 2 days.

Makes about 1 cup

Lovage Soup, Shrimp Toast

Lovage is an odd herb. Really a member of the celery family, it grows in profuse clumps, sending up bright green shoots early in the spring. It is these tender shoots that make the best soup. Later, the stalks get fibrous and tough, and the flavor becomes too sharp to mellow into a soup that pleases. You can probably find lovage at the farmers' market in the spring; if not, bring home a small pot from the nursery. It adapts to most soil conditions and seems to need little care, coming back each spring bigger and better than the year before.

4 shallots
2 tablespoons unsalted butter
2 cups chicken stock
2 to 4 cups loosely packed lovage leaves (can substitute spinach)
¾ cup chopped cooked shrimp
2 tablespoons mayonnaise
1 tablespoon chopped chives
4 slices baguette
2 tablespoons grated Parmigiano-Reggiano cheese
1 cup heavy cream

IN A LARGE POT, sauté the shallots in the butter until soft and translucent. Add the stock and lovage, bring to a boil, and cook for 10 minutes. Remove from the heat and cool slightly before puréeing in a food processor or blender. Strain through a China cap or fine-mesh strainer and return to the heat.

MEANWHILE, PREHEAT THE BROILER. Mix the shrimp, mayonnaise, and chives together in a small bowl and spread on the baguette slices.

Dust the tops with the grated cheese and slip under the hot broiler for 2 or 3 minutes, or until the toast is bubbly and golden.

WHEN THE SOUP IS HOT, whisk in the cream and stir for a few minutes while it heats. Serve hot with the toast on the side.

Serves 4

Smoky Potato Soup, Salmon Caviar

I've never "smoked" a potato. The secret to this soup is stock made from smoked chicken. At Seattle Supersmoke, Cyril does a masterful job with all things smoked. His chickens are big, plump Washington birds treated to a tender cure and carefully hung in his giant smoker. The stock from these birds has so much personality that pairing it with the simple flavor of the humble potato seems just and right. Naturally, you can use any kind of fish eggs for the righteous garnish; the pairing of sturgeon and salmon eggs makes for a really elegant bowl of soup.

1 medium onion, diced
7 cloves garlic, crushed
2 tablespoons unsalted butter
4 large potatoes, cooked, or 4 to 6 cups leftover mashed potatoes
4 cups smoky chicken stock
1 cup heavy cream
Salt
White pepper
3 ounces salmon caviar for garnish

IN A LARGE POT, sauté the onion and garlic in the butter until soft and translucent. Peel the potatoes and add to the pot along with the stock. Bring to a boil and cook for 10 minutes, then purée in a food processor or blender. Return the mixture to the pot and heat with the cream. Add salt and white pepper to taste. Serve hot, with a spoonful of salmon caviar on top.

Serves 6

Tools

THE RIGHT TOOLS ARE ABSOLUTELY ESSENTIAL WHEN IT COMES TO making anything. Carpentry, mechanics, and cooking all have particular tools designed for particular jobs. Having the right tool can make the difference between joy and regret.  KITCHEN GADGETS ALWAYS FASCINATED ME. I come from a long line of gadget collectors. My grandmother had drawers full, collected in her later years after the apex of her cooking days had passed. They were bought, I suspect, to assuage the years spent doing without. I always bought gadgets that I thought I would need if I were to tackle some intimidating cooking challenge—making croissants, for instance. In kitchen shops and catalogs, one sees the croissant cutter: a roller bar on a handle with triangular grids, it certainly looks efficient. This is just the kind of purchase the fledgling croissant maker can get suckered into. After all, the triangular grids look as though they'll work, and how comforting it would be to go into your first croissant expedition with this clever device. So what if it won't fit into any drawer or cupboard in your kitchen? So, after rearranging the entire contents of the kitchen to accommodate your new friend, you vow to make croissants . . . soon. WHEN I FINALLY *DID* START MAKING CROISSANTS, it was 5 a.m. and I needed a hundred in an hour. Following Julia Child's instructions to the *absolute* letter, I had made the pastry the night before. I rolled out the dough, and it took about fifteen seconds for it to dawn on me that the roller was not going to work because the triangular grids were not all the same depth, so they wouldn't cut through the pastry all the way. ▮▮ VROOM! IT TURNED OUT THAT USING A ROLLING PIZZA CUTTER is just as fast, if not faster, and it does a better job. ▮▮ LATER, TWO LADIES IN THE DINING ROOM, obviously pastry aficionados, told me that my croissants were the best they'd had since Gilbert in Paris. Returning to the kitchen, I silently vowed to diligently follow recipes more often. The croissant cutter went in the garage-sale box. ▮▮ I FUSS AND FUME if I can't find my zester when I need it; ditto an offset frosting paddle, the potato peeler, the fine-mesh strainer, and, of course, my little Sabatier paring knife, given to me by Jean Louis the night before he returned to Lyon. A zester is a cunning little tool designed to remove the outer peel of any citrus fruit in tiny, fine little shavings or wide, curly loops. These shavings are invaluable for adding the flavor of lemon to anything. Real lemon flavor comes from the oil in the skin, not the juice, and the zester takes just the outer layer, not the bitter white pith that can ruin the taste. Cakes, ice creams, salads, sauces, and dressings can all be jazzed wonderfully with zest. ▮▮ KNIVES, GOOD SHARP ONES, are the single most valuable tool in the kitchen. And most often, they are just what's missing. Some very grand and expensive kitchens are lacking this most rudimentary tool. Of course, it is impossible to have any fun in the kitchen with a dull knife. The recipe says "Chop a carrot," and there you are, no peeler, struggling to cut the carrot with a dull knife that quickly breaks it. That is when you think, "I can't cook. How do they make it look so easy on TV?" Well, a sharp knife makes all the difference. It's actually easier to cut yourself with a dull knife than a sharp one; a dull knife will roll off what you are trying to cut instead of cutting through it. The other key to not cutting yourself is to focus on what you're doing and go slowly. Real pros seldom cut themselves because they have learned this painful truth by cutting themselves so much! The knives you choose are important too. This doesn't mean you must invest in a set of those big, hunking German blades. I prefer very thin, lightweight blades with well-attached handles. The Japanese knives I use are inexpensive, well made, and easy to sharpen. When one disappears, I don't have to root through the Dumpster if I feel I have gotten enough years out of it. The German knives are great for splitting hairs—something we don't do much of in my kitchen.

Hot and Sour Fish Soup

The first time I made this soup, I created it solely from taste. I had had a bowl at a Vietnamese restaurant. At that time, Vietnamese places were new and rare. I had never seen any Vietnamese or Chinese recipes or cookbooks, though I suppose they were out there. I just loved the flavor so much I wanted to taste it again. I knew the base was chicken stock, and obviously there was vinegar and ginger. I used lime zest and lemon mint tea, trying to get that bright underlayment of flavor. It worked out okay, but after I discovered the Welcome Vietnamese Grocery my cooking changed forever. I just loved that little store, with its strange smells and scary bins of dried things. I would roam the narrow aisles with my cart for hours, reading labels or admiring the artwork on them, sniffing, squeezing. There, on my own, in the aisles of Welcome Grocery, I discovered pickled ginger, arame, fresh and dried lemon grass, galangal, fresh litchis, baby octopus, fermented black beans, rice wine vinegar, cane vinegar. I was fascinated by the different piles of noodles. The packages were often inscrutable, giving only the barest description of the contents. I loved the labels and was fascinated by how the things inside might be used. My recreation was blowing five dollars on interesting ingredients, then taking them home to play with. This exploration was all long before I became a professional chef. I was young and hungry for life, and for soup!

½ package (6 ounces) small wonton wrappers
3 green onions
1 bunch spinach, well washed, stems removed
4 cups chicken or fish stock
2 cloves garlic, chopped
2 tablespoons peeled, grated ginger
4 lime leaves
2 tablespoons nuoc mam *(fish sauce)*
1 cup seasoned rice wine vinegar

1 teaspoon crushed dried red chiles
1 to 2 cups large chunks cooked Dungeness crabmeat, rock fish, or halibut
1 carrot, julienned
Salt and freshly ground black pepper
Mint sprigs for garnish
Cilantro sprigs for garnish

CUT THE WONTON WRAPPERS IN HALF, cut the green onions on the diagonal, and tear the spinach leaves into bite-size pieces. In a large pot, bring the stock, garlic, ginger, and lime leaves to a boil, turn down the heat to a simmer, and cook for 20 minutes to let the flavors marry. Add the nuoc mam, rice wine vinegar, and crushed chiles. Taste for seasoning.

ADD THE WONTON WRAPPERS and cook for 2 minutes; add the crabmeat and heat through. Then add the carrot, spinach, and green onions. The heat of the soup will cook these instantly. Add salt and pepper to taste.

SERVE IMMEDIATELY, garnished with the mint and cilantro sprigs.

Serves 6

Mussel and Clam Chowder

I resisted serving chowder for years. I grew up eating clam chowder, and it just didn't seem special enough for my restaurant. Didn't everybody make it at home? My son finally convinced me that, no, they didn't, and most restaurant versions were so mediocre, I should take the opportunity to turn people on to real chowder; good chowder deserves a place in a fine seafood eatery. This recipe is almost exactly the way my mother and probably my grandmother made chowder; they just never used mussels. Add the cooked shellfish at the end, because both the clams and the mussels will get tough if cooked too long. The traditional bacon is missing, deliberately, making this a "fishetarian" chowder.

For the Shellfish

1 quart fresh, small clams
2 cups water
1 cup white wine
1 teaspoon freshly ground black pepper
2 cloves garlic, crushed
1 quart mussels, debearded, with clean, unbroken shells

IN A LARGE POT, steam the clams, water, wine, pepper, and garlic together for 10 minutes over high heat, or until the shells open. Remove the clams and use the cooking liquid to cook the mussels in exactly the same way. Drain the mussels and reserve the liquid. When cool, remove the mussels and clams from the shells and reserve the meat. Discard the shells.

For the Chowder

3 to 6 cloves garlic, crushed
1 onion, diced
3 stalks celery, diced
½ cup (1 stick) unsalted butter, melted
4 cups reserved cooking liquid
2 large russet potatoes, peeled and cut into ½-inch dice
2 carrots, diced
6 cups half-and-half
1 tablespoon fresh tarragon leaves, chopped, or 1 teaspoon dried
1 tablespoon fresh thyme leaves, chopped, or 1 teaspoon dried
¼ cup cornstarch
½ cup milk
Salt and freshly ground black pepper
½ cup chopped flat-leaf Italian parsley
2 tablespoons chopped chives

IN A LARGE POT, sauté the garlic, onion, and celery in the butter until soft. Add the reserved cooking liquid and the potatoes, bring to a boil, and cook for 10 minutes, then add the carrots and cook for 3 minutes more. Add the half-and-half, the clams and mussels, and the herbs and heat gently to boiling. In a small bowl, whisk together the cornstarch and milk. Add to the chowder, and continue whisking until the chowder is slightly thickened. Add salt and pepper to taste. Mix in the parsley and garnish with the chopped chives.

Serves 6 to 8

Cauliflower Soup

This soup has its origins in "The Cheese Tray." When I opened Christina's in the spring of 1980, I had the idea, gleaned from reading too much M. F. K. Fisher and Quentin Crewe, of offering a tray of cheeses for dessert. Please know that it was 1980, and my restaurant, while charming in its renovated waterfront location over the town gas pump (when it was time to begin serving dinner, I got them to turn off the pinger that rang when the cars drove through), was catering to a hoped-for clientele of casual summer vacationers, locals, and (I imagined) sophisticated world travelers. The fact that there were few good cheeses available was not going to stop me. I found an antique oak tea trolley and foraged for, bought, and borrowed three cheese domes and the little wooden boards that went underneath them. Each evening, before service, I would carefully arrange the cheeses under their little domes. The pleasure that I took from creating this homage to my dream of a great restaurant far outweighed the cost of the lost cheeses, which sat, elegant and aloof, night after night under their little domes, decaying oh so beautifully.

Since that time, the food world has shifted on its axis, and we have wonderful cheeses to serve from Washington State and all over the world. And what's really great is that people order it.

All cheeses are fair game for this soup. Don't be shy. It's only soup.

1 medium sweet onion, chopped
3 tablespoons unsalted butter
1 large head cauliflower
2 cups chicken stock
4 to 6 ounces cheese
3 cups heavy cream
White pepper
Salt
Freshly grated nutmeg for garnish

IN A LARGE POT, sauté the onion in the butter for a few minutes, until soft and translucent. Break or cut the cauliflower into pieces and add to the pot, along with the chicken stock. Bring to a boil and cook over high heat for 15 minutes, until the cauliflower is soft, then add the cheese, grated or cut into small cubes, and whisk until melted. Purée the soup in a food processor or blender until smooth. Return to the pot and heat gently, whisking in the cream. Taste and season with white pepper and salt. Grate fresh nutmeg on top and serve hot.

Serves 4 to 6

Main Courses

Rockfish, Chips, Piccalilli Tartar

Saffron-Poached Halibut, Fava Beans, Shallots

Copper River King Salmon, Seaweed Rice, Shoyu Butter

Planked King Salmon, Lemon Radish Vinaigrette

Roasted Halibut, Potato Sorrel Hash, Sweet Pepper Butter

Sockeye, Champagne Cream, Steamed Potatoes

Halibut Cheeks, Smoked Tomato Jus, Bright Lights Chard, Big Couscous

Roasted Halibut, Basil Glaze

Wasp Passage Seafood Stew

Lucky New Year's Gumbo

Grilled Sturgeon, Blueberry Chutney

Ling Cod, Mustard Caper Glaze, Thyme-Roasted Yukon Golds

Pepper Crab Hot Pot

Lamb Shanks, Flageolets, Root Vegetables

Mixed Grill, Juniper Aïoli

Filet of Beef, Gorgonzola Sherry Cream, Horseradish Potatoes Gratin

Pomegranate Lamb Chops, Rhubarb Mint Chutney

Lamb and Morel Ragout, Shallots and Gold Beets

Rib-Eye Steak, Mushrooms, Alice Waters' Onion Rings

Braised Short Ribs, Spicy Sweet Potatoes

New York Steak, Tipsy Onion Butter, Fatso Mashed Potatoes

Sage-Roasted Chicken, Porcini Bread Pudding

Smoked Paprika Chicken, Corn Pudding

Spring Vegetable Pot Pie

Rabbit Stew, Sage Dumplings

Three Raviolis

Roast Pheasant, Pumpkin Risotto, Black Walnut Gremolata

Halibut Cheeks, Smoked Tomato Jus, Bright Lights Chard, Big Couscous, page 150

Rockfish, Chips, Piccalilli Tartar

The first time I caught a rockfish, I could hardly believe my eyes. The spiny, bug-eyed creature I pulled from the depths was so ugly, and the adults in the boat seemed to be terrified. To a chorus of shouted cautions, my brother removed the salmon lure and pitched the shimmering fish over the side. As I watched the fish swim away, I could see how beautiful he really was.

Rockfish was peddled as red snapper in the Pacific Northwest for years, but savvy buyers have changed all that, and the once lowly creature has taken its place among the ranks of the great-eating fish. Fish batters, for me, are all about lightness and crunch. This simple method provides both.

For the Piccalilli Tartar

> 2 cups mayonnaise, homemade (see page 8) or purchased
> 1 cup Piccalilli Relish (see page 13)
> 1 tablespoon capers
> 1 teaspoon fresh lemon juice

MIX ALL THE INGREDIENTS TOGETHER IN a bowl. Refrigerate until ready to use. The sauce will keep, refrigerated, for up to 10 days.

Makes 3 cups

> 2 pounds rockfish
> 1 cup buttermilk
> 2 russet potatoes
> 3 cups peanut oil for frying
> 2 cups unbleached white flour
> ½ cup cornstarch
> 1 teaspoon salt
> ½ teaspoon white pepper
> 1 tablespoon paprika

CUT THE ROCKFISH INTO 12 PIECES, all about the same size, and place in a large bowl with the buttermilk.

CUT THE POTATOES INTO THIN SLICES about ⅛ inch thick. Put the sliced potatoes in a second bowl and cover with cold water. Let the potatoes soak for at least 1 hour. This removes some of the starch and makes the potatoes crisper after they're cooked.

PLACE THE OIL IN A DEEP POT and heat it to 365°F. Mix the flour, cornstarch, salt, white pepper, and paprika in a third bowl and dredge the pieces of fish in this mixture. Fry them in the oil, a few pieces at a time, until they are crispy and golden, about 4 minutes. Remove from the oil with a slotted spoon and drain on a paper towel. Use a thermometer to make sure the oil returns to 365°F between batches.

DRAIN THE POTATO SLICES IN A COLANDER and pat dry with a towel before putting them into the hot oil. To prevent burns, use a long-handled mesh or slotted spoon for placing them in and removing them from the hot oil. Arrange the rockfish and potatoes on serving plates, and serve with piccalilli tartar.

Serves 4

Saffron-Poached Halibut, Fava Beans, Shallots

After eating poached turbot for lunch at the fabled Jamin in Paris, I was burning to cook. The following Saturday I shopped the market in Le Vesinet with my pals Charles and Laurana and bought everything I needed. That night, for a dinner party at their home, I re-created my lunch at Jamin, down to the tiny little onion rings that drifted as garnish in the pale yellow broth.

½ teaspoon loose saffron threads
3 cups fish stock
1 cup good, fruity white wine
2 tablespoons pear vinegar or other bright flavored vinegar
12 smallest red or fingerling potatoes, cooked
4 halibut fillets, 4 to 6 ounces each
1 cup shelled fava beans (or substitute shelled peas)
4 shallots, thinly sliced
½ cup buttermilk
Seasoned unbleached white flour for dredging
Oil for sautéing

BEGIN BY GENTLY TOASTING THE SAFFRON THREADS in a sauté pan over low heat for a few minutes to dry them out and release their flavor. Transfer the threads to a mortar with a pestle or, if you don't have a mortar and pestle, use the back of a small spoon to grind the saffron threads to a fine powder in a small bowl. In a large saucepan, combine the stock with the wine and vinegar and bring to a gentle simmer. Add the saffron and cook for a few minutes. Add the potatoes and continue cooking until the potatoes are heated through, about 2 minutes. Add the fish fillets and the fava beans and simmer for 5 minutes. Place a lid on the pot and remove from the heat to finish cooking.

MARINATE, DREDGE, AND COOK THE SHALLOTS, following the instructions for preparing onion rings on page 74. Because shallots are small, they can be sautéed in a little oil in a sauté pan.

SERVE THE FILLETS IN SHALLOW BOWLS with the favas, potatoes, and saffron broth. Float a few of the shallot rings on the top as garnish. Serve immediately.

Serves 4

Chef's Tip: Fava beans show up at the markets in the spring. Here in the San Juan Islands, some farmers grow them as a winter cover crop to put nutrients back in the soil. To shell fava beans, split the pods lengthwise and scoop out the beans with your thumb. Drop the beans into boiling water and let them cook for 1 minute. Drain and chill. Remove the grayish husk from each bean by opening it at the seam.

Copper River King Salmon, Seaweed Rice, Shoyu Butter

The Copper River king salmon has achieved mythic status, not just in the Pacific Northwest but around the world. Before the PR campaign that created a "special" fish, the big, bright orange, net-caught, on-their-way-to-spawn salmon that showed up in the market every spring were known only to fishermen, a few brokers, and a few chefs. And now every year the price goes higher.

For the Salmon

6 fillets king or sockeye salmon, preferably fresh and wild caught,
   6 ounces each
Good-quality olive oil for brushing
Salt
1 green onion, finely julienned and soaked in ice water for 10 minutes

PLACE THE FILLETS IN A SHEET PAN, brush with olive oil to moisten them, and salt lightly. Set the pan aside until the fish is ready to cook. Hold the julienned onion for garnishing.

For the Rice

4 cups water
2 cups jasmine rice
1 teaspoon salt
1 teaspoon sugar
2 tablespoons arame or other dried seaweed, broken into small pieces
½ large carrot, cut into a ¹⁄₁₆-inch dice
½ medium zucchini, cut into a ¹⁄₁₆-inch dice

PREHEAT THE OVEN TO 450°F. Bring the water to a boil in a medium-size oven-safe pot. Add the rice and salt, bring the water back to a boil, and cover with a lid. Steam in the oven for 30 minutes, or until the water is absorbed and the rice is plump and sticky. In a bowl, toss the steaming rice with the sugar, arame, and vegetables. Set aside in a warm place until needed.

For the Shoyu Butter

> ¼ cup rice wine vinegar
> 1 lime leaf, crumbled
> 1 walnut-sized piece of ginger, peeled and chopped
> 1 tablespoon tamarind paste
> ½ medium onion, chopped
> 2 to 4 cloves garlic, mashed
> 1 cup orange juice
> ⅓ cup low-salt Japanese soy sauce
> 1 cup (2 sticks) very cold unsalted butter, cut into chunks
> 1 to 2 tablespoons brown sugar

IN A SAUCEPAN, MIX THE VINEGAR with the lime leaf, ginger, tamarind paste, onion, and garlic. Reduce until almost dry. Add the orange juice and reduce by half. Add the soy sauce, bring to a boil, and reduce only slightly. Whisk in the cold chunks of butter until smooth. Remove from the heat before all the butter has been incorporated. Add brown sugar to taste and continue whisking until the sauce is smooth. Keep warm until ready to serve.

To Serve

PREHEAT THE OVEN TO 400°F. Roast the salmon for 7 to 10 minutes, or until it is firm to the touch. Serve on heated plates with the rice and shoyu butter. Garnish with the julienned green onion.

Serves 6

Salmon

SALMON WAS "POOR FOOD." SMOKED, CANNED, OR PICKLED, IT WAS A diet mainstay for lots of island families. People in the San Juans really did live off the land and from the sea, right through the 1960s. There was a saying that as long as the tide went in and out, folks wouldn't starve. Today, the menu of fresh fish, clams, oysters, venison, lamb, apples, and berries that I serve in my restaurant is very much like what islanders were eating for most of the last century. I first came to Orcas with my parents, and they came to fish. In the early fifties the waters of Puget Sound were still abundant feeding grounds for salmon. It was easy to find fish. All you had to do was scan the horizon with the binoculars until you found the cloud of seagulls. If you followed them, you would arrive to a melee of birds whooping and calling as they fed on the herring ball just beneath the surface. The salmon were feeding on the herring, and the seals were feeding on the salmon, and, if it was a *really* great day, the orcas were feeding on the seals. We would troll through the middle of all this activity in the little green boat from Curly Cramer's West Beach Cabins and reel in fish after fish. One year, as we trolled up Presidents Channel on the northwest shore of Orcas, we watched as two purse seiners worked in tandem, laying their nets across the entire channel between Waldron and Orcas. My father was furious and stood in our little boat and yelled to the men on board that if they kept it up there wouldn't be any fish left. They just laughed and waved us away. ❚❘❚ IN THE FIFTY YEARS SINCE, king salmon has been designated an endangered species in Washington State. Alaska has managed its salmon runs far better than anyplace else and has maintained its wild salmon population, but here officials were lulled into complacency, believing that the hatcheries they built would be enough to keep the salmon population viable. It took forty years to figure out that a genetically nondiverse hatchery fish didn't have the same strength as the wild fish and thus lacked the ability to survive in the wild and return to its spawning ground. ❚❘❚ ISLANDER JIM YOUNGREN STARTED HIS OWN HATCHERY at Glenwood Springs on Orcas Island in the 1970s. His encounter with some aged fishermen at Neah Bay in his youth had left a lasting impression: tales of salmon so thick in rivers you could pick the one you wanted, or the smell of the dying fish three feet deep on the banks of the Stillaguamish, or of just sitting in your boat and watching the fish leap in, as if they were climbing rapids, were part of our heritage. Youngren's hatchery was ignored by the state until he sought permission to donate, for fund-raising purposes, some of the giant kings that had begun to return. The state's response to the quantity of fish returning to Jim's hatchery was to let the purse seiners fish in East Sound bay, which hadn't had a commercial salmon season in over sixty years. Now the organization that Youngren founded, Long Live the Kings, has some good funding and continues its work of rebuilding the wild salmon runs of Puget Sound. ❚❘❚ NEIGHBORHOODS THROUGHOUT

SEATTLE are designated watersheds, and whole communities come out to cheer the salmon as they make their way upstream to spawn. Here in the San Juans we are working to protect the eelgrass, damaged by dock building, which is where the herring spawn. Since contaminated groundwater and silt are the biggest threat to healthy creeks and rivers, in the Pacific Northwest we are conscientious about what we put on our lawns and wash down our storm drains. Meanwhile, Alaska has an abundance of wild salmon. The season and the catch are so well managed that troll-caught kings are available at Seattle's Pike Place Market a good six months of the year. 🕚 FARMED SALMON IS AVAILABLE YEAR-ROUND and is extremely fresh: It isn't pulled out of the pond until it is ordered. Restaurants are happy to have it, especially here in the Northwest, where restaurant-goers hope to dine on salmon year-round. However, the difference between wild, troll-caught salmon and farm-raised fish is huge. The color is the most obvious difference to the casual observer. Farm-raised fish are colored by a material that is added to their diet to give them that famous pink color. Wild salmon that have fed in the ocean have a deep red color that comes from feeding on brine shrimp. Wild fish are also healthier, with better flavor and higher fat content. Farm-raised fish aren't real salmon; they are a species from the Atlantic that is very different from our Northwest kings. Instead, eat wild-caught salmon in season, cook it lightly, and make a toast with good Northwest pinot gris: "Long live the kings!"

Planked King Salmon, Lemon Radish Vinaigrette

Quite a bit of fluff has been written about the planking of salmon. I have never seen the Northwest native peoples cook salmon by planking it. The Lummi people, also known as the Salmon People, cook salmon by threading fillets on long sticks and sticking them in the ground vertically around a fire, which is usually huge, roaring, and hot. The salmon fillets are at least 2 feet away from the fire. This also makes the best salmon I have ever had. When I talked to the fish maestro about his methods, he told me the sticks had been his grandfather's and he thought they might be oak. They were very dark—from oil, he said—and very smooth, and each was about 6 feet long. The Lummis heavily salt the fish a few hours before cooking. The maestro added, "They come from salt; they go to salt."

Planking is fun, though, and the cedar imparts a vague woodsy flavor. You don't need a fancy cured piece of cedar. I use shingles. Make sure they don't have any stain or oil on them, and when the edges start to smoke a little in the oven, well, there's the woodsy flavoring.

For the Vinaigrette

Grated zest and juice of 1 lemon
¼ cup sherry vinegar
1 tablespoon sugar
½ cup fruity extra virgin olive oil
4 medium radishes, cut into matchsticks
3 tablespoons chopped flat-leaf Italian parsley
1 tablespoon whole red peppercorns
Salt
Freshly ground black pepper

WHISK TOGETHER all the ingredients in a bowl and set aside.

Note: The vinaigrette will keep in the refrigerator for a week, but it will lose its color, as the acid in the lemon and vinegar will "cook" the parsley and radish.

For the Salmon

4 king salmon fillets, 6 to 8 ounces each, skin on
Good-quality olive oil for brushing
Salt
Lemon wedges for garnish

PREHEAT THE OVEN TO 400°F. LACE the salmon fillets skin side down on a cedar plank or cedar shingle. Brush with olive oil, and sprinkle with salt to your liking.

ROAST THE SALMON ON THE PLANKS for 10 minutes, or until the salmon is firm to the touch. Remove the salmon from the plank by slipping a spatula between the fish and the skin. If the fish is done, the meat will separate easily from the skin.

SERVE THE SALMON HOT, with the vinaigrette ladled over it and garnish with lemon wedges.

Serves 4

Roasted Halibut, Potato Sorrel Hash, Sweet Pepper Butter

Fifty-, sixty-, and seventy-pound halibut are not that uncommon. Since they're deepwater fish, the cold provides them with a sheet of glistening fat that flavors the meat and makes for moist, easy cooking. Fresh halibut is deeply opalescent: When you touch it, there is a delicate jiggle.

We had a huge surplus of sorrel when we came up with this entrée. If you don't have access to sorrel, the recipe is also wonderful with spinach, arugula, or even pea vines. Taste the sauce after you have put the butter in it and decide whether you might like to add that teaspoon of sugar. Every sweet pepper has its own personality; if it's not sweet enough on its own, give it a little nudge.

For the Sweet Pepper Butter

⅓ cup white balsamic vinegar
2 cloves garlic, finely chopped
2 shallots, finely chopped
½ cup white wine
1 to 1½ cups (2 to 3 sticks) very cold unsalted butter
1 red bell pepper, roasted (see page 115), peeled, seeded, and puréed
1 teaspoon sugar (optional)
Salt

IN A MEDIUM SAUCEPAN, combine the vinegar with the garlic and shallots and reduce until there are 1 or 2 tablespoons left in the pan. Add the wine and reduce again until 2 or 3 tablespoons of liquid remain. Break the cold butter into pieces and whisk piece by piece into the boiling reduction, adding the next piece before the previous piece has been totally incorporated into the sauce. When half the butter has been used, add all the puréed red pepper, whisking constantly. Since peppers vary in their sweetness and depth of flavor, taste the mixture and determine how much more butter to add. The sauce should be intensely flavored—more sweet pepper than butter. Add salt to taste. Strain the sauce and keep in a warm, but not hot, place.

For the Halibut

4 halibut fillets, 6 to 8 ounces each, skin on
Unsalted butter, melted, for brushing
Salt

PREHEAT THE OVEN TO 400°F. Place the halibut in a sheet pan. Brush with butter and sprinkle with salt. Roast for 7 to 10 minutes, until the halibut is firm to the touch.

For the Hash

1 large red onion, cut into ½-inch dice
3 tablespoons unsalted butter, melted
4 large russet potatoes, cooked, peeled, and cut into ¼-inch chunks
2 large carrots, cooked and cut into ½-inch dice
1 teaspoon dried tarragon
1 teaspoon dried oregano
2 tablespoons chopped flat-leaf Italian parsley
4 cups whole sorrel leaves, cut into ¾- to 1-inch pieces
1½ teaspoons salt
½ teaspoon freshly ground black pepper

WITH THE OVEN STILL SET AT 400°F, in a large sauté pan, sauté the onion in 1 tablespoon of the butter until soft and translucent. Add the potatoes, carrots, tarragon, oregano, parsley, and the remaining 2 tablespoons butter. Transfer to a shallow pan and roast for 7 minutes or so. Toss the mixture around a few times to keep the butter distributed. Remove from the oven, add the sorrel, salt, and pepper, and toss until the sorrel wilts.

To Serve

SERVE THE HALIBUT ATOP A SPOONFUL of the hash, surrounded by the pepper butter.

Serves 4

Sockeye, Champagne Cream, Steamed Potatoes

In the early years of my career as a chef, I read anything and everything I could get my hands on about successful restaurants and chefs. I was sitting in the dentist's office when I read a long and thoughtful essay in *Smithsonian* magazine about Le Bernadin, a restaurant in New York City that was just coming on the scene. Gilbert Le Coze was the young Frenchman in charge of the kitchen. His sister ran the dining room. The article marveled at the restaurant's use of fresh fish and produce from a "real" garden. I thought, "What's the big deal? We've been doing that since we opened." Of course, my restaurant was on Orcas Island in the far northwest corner of Washington, and Le Bernardin was in New York. But we were both on the cusp of the same food revolution. At the end of the article was a recipe for a reduced cream sauce served over poached oysters. All I remember is that it called for 4 ounces of smoked haddock. In the years since, I have fiddled with this idea endlessly, using everything in the reduction, from champagne to Jack Daniel's, chardonnay, sherry vinegar, rice wine vinegar, and even smoked oysters. But I've never used smoked haddock. Gilbert was one of the great ones. He died too young, before I ever had the chance to thank him.

For the Champagne Cream

½ cup champagne vinegar
2 shallots, finely chopped
2 cloves garlic, minced
3-ounce piece of smoked salmon, whole
¾ cup champagne
1 cup heavy cream

IN A MEDIUM SAUCEPAN, combine the champagne vinegar with the shallots, garlic, and smoked salmon and reduce to about 1 tablespoon. Add the champagne and reduce again until there are about 2 tablespoons of liquid left in the pan. Add the cream and reduce slightly until the cream thickens and the bubbles get big. Reserve and keep warm.

For the Steamed Potatoes

8 small Red Bliss or Nordland potatoes
Salt

IN A POT WITH A TIGHT-FITTING LID, put the potatoes in about 2 inches of water. Salt the water well and boil with the lid on for 20 minutes, or until a potato slides cleanly off the fork.

For the Salmon

4 salmon fillets, 6 to 8 ounces each
Unsalted butter, melted, for brushing
Salt
Chives for garnish

PREHEAT THE OVEN TO 400°F. Brush the salmon fillets with melted butter, and sprinkle with salt to your liking. Place in a sheet pan and roast for 10 minutes, or until the fish is firm and slightly crisp at the edges. Serve surrounded by the sauce, and garnish with the steamed potatoes and chives.

Serves 4

Halibut Cheeks, Smoked Tomato Jus, Bright Lights Chard, Big Couscous

What I say on my menu is "Halibut Cheeks with Chard and Couscous." Let the smoked tomato jus be a surprise. Ditto the chard with the ribald stems. The sweet part of this recipe is the halibut cheeks, a delicacy that for years was known only to the halibut fishermen and natives of Alaska's Inside Passage. Luckily for me, the "last of the millionaire playboys" was, in his early days, a halibut fisherman! He cooked with a cigar in his mouth and a frilly apron over his midsection, and he held a glass of (usually) red wine in his hand. He made me some very fine meals.

For the Smoked Tomato Jus

3 cups fish or chicken stock
½ cup white wine
1 tablespoon smoked paprika
1 cup tomato juice

COMBINE THE STOCK, wine, smoked paprika, and tomato juice in a saucepan and simmer over medium heat for a few minutes so that the flavors marry. Reserve.

For the Couscous

1 medium red onion, chopped
3 cloves garlic, finely chopped
2 tablespoons good-quality olive oil
2½ cups chicken stock or water
1 teaspoon salt
6 leaves and stems of multicolored Swiss chard
2 cups Israeli couscous

IN A MEDIUM SAUCEPAN, sauté the onion and garlic in the oil for a few minutes, until soft and translucent. Add the stock and salt and bring to a boil. Chop the Swiss chard into pieces: cut the stems into 1-inch pieces, and cut the leaves larger. When the stock is boiling, add the couscous and Swiss chard. Immediately remove from the heat and cover with foil or a tight-fitting lid.

18 small to medium halibut cheeks
½ cup chopped fresh mint

WHILE THE COUSCOUS MIXTURE STEAMS, bring the smoked tomato jus to a boil. Reduce the heat to a simmer and add the halibut cheeks; cover with a lid and let the cheeks poach for 1 minute. Remove from the heat.

ADD HALF THE MINT to the couscous and chard, toss together, and place a large spoonful of the couscous in each deep bowl. Remove the halibut cheeks from the jus with a slotted spoon and place three on the couscous in each bowl. Pour the smoked tomato jus around the couscous and garnish with the rest of the mint. Serve immediately.

Serves 6

Chef's Tip: Adding the fresh herbs just before you serve a dish ensures the brightest flavor and best color. The heat gently releases the flavor and softens the texture of the herbs.

Roasted Halibut, Basil Glaze

I was so culinarily naive when I started cooking professionally, I thought my idea for basil glaze was something new. *Sauce verte* is a classic French cold mayonnaise made with capers, watercress, parsley, anchovies, and garlic. I had been making it a lot in the summer to go with cold poached salmon, but then the watercress dried up, literally—the creek I was getting it from dried up! Substituting basil wasn't a giant leap, but holy cow! The flavor! I started smearing it on everything. A reviewer said it would make spark plugs taste good. As time went by, I started leaving out more and more of the classic *sauce verte* ingredients. Finally I was using just basil, garlic, and homemade mayonnaise. This combination turns a luminous green when exposed to heat for a minute or two.

6 pieces halibut, 4 to 6 ounces each, skin on
Good-quality olive oil for brushing
Salt
2 cups Homemade Mayonnaise (see page 8)
2 cups basil leaves
2 tablespoons Bar U Ranch Mustard (see page 7)
4 cloves roasted garlic (see page 108)
Roasted Vegetable Salad (see page 74), minus the vinaigrette dressing

PREHEAT THE OVEN TO 400°F. Place the halibut in a sheet pan. Brush it with olive oil, and sprinkle with salt to your liking. Put the mayonnaise, basil, mustard, and garlic in a food processor or blender and purée until smooth. Roast the halibut for 7 to 10 minutes, until the fish feels firm to the touch. Remove from the oven and put a generous tablespoon of basil mayonnaise on top of each fillet. Return to the oven for 1 minute or so, until the mayonnaise "glazes" and turns bright green. Remove from the oven and serve immediately on top of the Roasted Vegetable Salad.

Serves 6

Wasp Passage Seafood Stew

Old timers described the narrow passage through the rocks on the southwest corner of Orcas as "shaped like a wasp." Now charted as Wasp Passage, the rocky shore's deep cold water is home to many varieties of rockfish, cod, and the rich Dungeness crab. Our crabman Drew Sandilands sets his pots there during the season.

Real bouillabaisse, the classic French fisherman's soup, can't really be made anywhere but the south of France. The defining fish, rascasse, a bony little specimen with a particular oily flavor, is part of the incidental day's catch in that region. Fishermen keep all the odds and ends that appear in their nets and use them to make bouillabaisse, a mixture of what's left over. So even though I have made various incarnations of this seafood stew, it has never been "real" bouillabaisse. The classic accompaniment is rouille. Meaning "rust" in English, it is named for its color, which comes from the sweet and spicy red peppers.

1 medium onion, chopped
6 cloves garlic, minced
2 tablespoons good-quality olive oil
1 cup white wine
6 cups fish stock
4 tomatoes, peeled, seeded, and chopped
1 teaspoon ground cumin
1 teaspoon dried basil
1 teaspoon dried oregano
1 teaspoon dried tarragon
6 ounces rockfish, cut into 1-ounce chunks
6 ounces salmon, cut into 1-ounce chunks
6 ounces ling cod, cut into 1-ounce chunks
2 quarts small steamer clams
2 quarts mussels, cleaned and debearded
18 small red potatoes, cooked

2 Dungeness crabs, cleaned and cracked in pieces
½ cup Pernod, or to taste
Salt and freshly ground black pepper
½ cup chopped flat-leaf Italian parsley
1½ cups Rouille (see page 61)
Sliced baguettes, for serving

IN A LARGE SOUP POT, sauté the onion and garlic in the oil until soft and translucent. Deglaze the pan with the wine by pouring it over the onion while the pan is hot and scraping up the bits of garlic and onion. Add the stock, tomatoes, and cumin. Rub the dried herbs in the palm of your hand to release the flavor before you add them to the pot. Simmer for 20 minutes or so over medium heat.

IN RAPID SUCCESSION, layer in the seafood and potatoes, starting with the chunks of fish, then the clams, mussels, potatoes, and crab on top. Add Pernod and salt and pepper to taste. Cover with a lid and steam for 5 minutes, just until the clams and mussels open. Add the chopped parsley and ladle the fish and shellfish into warm bowls. Rouille is a traditional accompaniment to bouillabaise. Individual ramekins of rouille allow for dipping the pieces of fish and shellfish. Have sliced baguettes on hand for dipping into the broth as well.

Serves 6

Lucky New Year's Gumbo

Gumbo is Creole for "stew." And it doesn't necessarily include okra or gumbo file, a seasoning concoction made with sassafras. I learned how to make gumbo by reading the great Paul Prudhomme. His book *Louisiana Kitchen* has a whole section on the Cajun-style roux that is the hallmark of the fabulous soups and stews created by Prudhomme in his namesake New Orleans restaurant. As soon as I mastered Prudhomme's roux technique, I veered off in my own direction, taking his method and his "holy trinity"—sweet peppers, onion, and celery—with me. If you cook in your head, as I do, this is the kind of recipe that confounds—such simple ingredients, and not many of them. Where does the miraculous flavor come from? Do not be fooled by the small number of peppers. This bowl has the perfect amount of heat—deep, rich flavor, intensified by the pepper but not buried by it. Even though it's hot, you just want another spoonful, and another. Thank you, Paul.

½ cup peanut oil
½ cup unbleached white flour
1 bay leaf, crumbled
1 teaspoon finely chopped garlic
½ teaspoon freshly ground black pepper
½ teaspoon cayenne pepper
½ teaspoon white pepper
1 large red onion, cut into ¼-inch dice
1 large red bell pepper, seeded and cut into ¼-inch dice
2 stalks celery, cut into ¼-inch dice
6 cups chicken stock
1 pound kielbasa, andouille, or other spicy smoked sausage, cooked, cut in ½-inch slices
4 large leaves black kale, Swiss chard, or other savory green
24 large spot prawns or other shrimp

IN A LARGE, DEEP FRYING PAN, heat the peanut oil over medium-high heat for 3 minutes or so, until it is very hot. Dump in the flour all at once, whisking constantly. Keep whisking until the flour just begins to turn a light tan color. Add the bay leaf and garlic and whisk for another 40 seconds. Add the black, cayenne, and white peppers all at once and keep whisking as you add the onion, red pepper, and celery. Blend as best you can, and remove from the heat. This is the roux.

IN A SOUP POT, heat the chicken stock and add the roux. Whisk well and simmer for 20 minutes or so. Add the cooked sausage and the kale. Just before you are ready to serve, add the shrimp and cook until they are pink and firm, about 4 minutes. Serve immediately in warm bowls.

Serves 6

Grilled Sturgeon, Blueberry Chutney

In case you haven't heard, we are all on a wild-sturgeon hiatus, to give the depleted species a chance to recover. Sturgeon abuse has run rampant overseas, and now it has spread to the United States. Wild-eyed Russian mafiosi have been caught wading in the irrigation ditches of California, armed with clubs and toting sacks. Fortunately, clever fish farmers have started raising sturgeon domestically. Their flavor isn't as delicate as that of wild sturgeon, naturally, but they are good, and very good for grilling.

> *4 sturgeon fillets, 6 to 8 ounces each*
> *Good-quality olive oil for brushing*
> *Salt*
> *¼ cup Blueberry Chutney (see page 18)*

LIGHT A MEDIUM-HOT FIRE in a charcoal grill, or preheat a gas grill. Brush the sturgeon fillets lightly with the oil (too much oil and the grill will smoke, leaving a black film on the fish). Salt the fish on both sides and grill for 2 to 3 minutes per side, or until the fish is firm. Serve warm, with the Blueberry Chutney on the side.

Serves 4

Ling Cod, Mustard Caper Glaze, Thyme-Roasted Yukon Golds

Not only have I made this at Christina's, I have served it for dinner parties at home as well. Like everyone else, I want to schmooze with my friends when I entertain. This recipe requires little supervision and can almost be made in advance. I give Pierre Franey, the legendary chef, some credit for the glaze; he it got from an East Hampton hostess. He couldn't figure out what she had done and was astonished when she confided her simple secret. In an effort to make it more complex, I added the capers.

> *1½ cups Homemade Mayonnaise (see page 8)*
> *⅔ cup whole-grain mustard*
> *2 tablespoons capers, rinsed and drained*
> *6 pieces ling cod, 4 to 6 ounces each, bones removed*
> *12 small Yukon Gold potatoes, cooked for 15 minutes in rapidly boiling*
> *   salted water, then drained and chilled*
> *Unsalted butter, melted, for brushing*
> *Salt*
> *1 tablespoon fresh thyme leaves*
> *Chopped chives for garnish*

PREHEAT THE OVEN TO 400°F. In a small bowl, whisk together the mayonnaise, mustard, and capers. Place the ling cod fillets in a shallow roasting pan and arrange the cooked potatoes around them. Brush the fish and potatoes with butter, sprinkle with salt and thyme, and roast for 10 to 12 minutes, until the cod feels firm to the touch and the butter has just begun to brown. Remove from the oven and preheat the broiler. Spread a little of the mustard mixture on top of each piece of fish. Place under the broiler for a minute or so, until the mustard sets. Sprinkle the fillets with the chives and serve immediately on a platter with the roasted potatoes.

Serves 6

Pepper Crab Hot Pot

My father always ordered Tomato Curry Noodles at the China Lantern. My mom had Almond Chicken. Billy, my brother, ate fried shrimp. I had a cheeseburger. When I finally did taste my dad's noodles, I never forgot them. The heat of the curry is cut by the acid of the sweet tomatoes and the brightness of the lime. I quit adding the noodles years ago. They just got tangled up with the crab legs.

> 1 medium red onion, chopped
> 8 cloves garlic, chopped
> ¼ cup peanut oil
> 2 to 4 tablespoons curry powder
> 3 cups crab stock (see Crab Bisque, page 112)
> 3 cups beef stock
> 3 lime leaves
> 1 cup tomato juice
> 3 ripe tomatoes, peeled, seeded, and chopped
> 2 tablespoons chopped cilantro
> ¼ cup rice wine vinegar
> 1 tablespoon peeled, grated ginger
> 1 teaspoon crushed dried red chiles
> 1 teaspoon cayenne (optional)
> 4 Dungeness crabs, cleaned and cracked

IN A DEEP SOUP POT, sauté the onion and garlic in the peanut oil until soft and translucent. Add the curry powder and cook 30 seconds longer. Add the crab and beef stocks, lime leaves, and tomato juice. Bring to a boil and cook for 5 minutes, then add the tomatoes, cilantro, vinegar, ginger, chiles, and cayenne, if using. Add the pieces of crab to the pot, heat them through, and serve in big bowls with crab crackers.

Serves 6 to 8

Lamb Shanks, Flageolets, Root Vegetables

As the granddaughter of a cattle rancher, I never tasted lamb until I was well into my twenties. Being wined and dined by the "last of the millionaire playboys" was an education, and I grew to love good lamb, especially when a bottle of something *noir*ish that tasted of earth and the joy of peasant toil came up from his cellar. This dish is how everybody used to cook: build a blazing fire in the morning, have coffee and maybe a bowl of gruel, put the meal in a pot in the oven, damp the fire down, and go outside and work until two or three in the afternoon. Then come inside and sit down to dinner. Braising is easy; the key is not to let the oven get too hot. The braising liquid should never boil. If the meat gets too hot, the cartilage breaks down and loses too much juice and goes stringy. If the beans seem a little too fey, this meal is great with mashed potatoes too.

2 tablespoons oil
Salt and freshly ground black pepper
6 lamb shanks
½ cup red wine
1 medium onion, finely chopped
2 tablespoons finely minced garlic
8 juniper berries
3 cups beef or lamb stock
¼ cup balsamic vinegar
¼ cup maple syrup
2 sprigs rosemary, each 3 inches long, plus more for garnish
2 sprigs thyme, each 2 inches long, plus more for garnish
1½ cups uncooked flageolets, cannellini, or other tasty, large beans
1 cup pearl onions, blanched and peeled
3 leeks, split, trimmed, and cut into 2-inch lengths
2 beets, cooked, peeled, and cut into wedges

1 turnip, peeled and cut into 6 wedges
2 parsnips, peeled and cut into 2-inch pieces
2 carrots, peeled and cut into 2-inch pieces

PREHEAT THE OVEN TO 275°F. In a large, heavy frying or roasting pan, heat the oil. Salt and pepper the lamb shanks well and brown in the oil, turning to obtain a golden-brown crust on all sides.

MEANWHILE, IN A MEDIUM SAUCEPAN, combine the wine, onion, garlic, and juniper berries and boil until reduced by half. Add the stock, vinegar, and maple syrup. Cook for a few minutes more and remove from the heat.

PLACE THE BROWNED LAMB SHANKS in a deep casserole or roasting pan that has a lid or that can be covered tightly with foil. Place the rosemary and thyme sprigs between the shanks. Pour the stock mixture over the shanks and seal with a lid or foil. Braise in the oven for 3½ hours.

MEANWHILE, BRING 6 CUPS OF WATER TO A BOIL and pour it over the flageolets in a large bowl. Let the beans sit for 1 hour, then drain.

REMOVE THE SHANKS FROM THE OVEN after 1½ hours and move them to the side of the pan or stack them to make a place for the beans in the stock. Make sure the beans are covered with the stock then reseal the lid and return to the oven. The shanks need not be immersed in the liquid to braise.

WHEN THERE IS ½ HOUR LEFT for the lamb to braise, add all the root vegetables and reseal the lid tightly. Cook until the vegetables are tender, about ½ hour more.

SERVE THE LAMB SHANKS HOT on a platter or on individual plates with the beans and the root vegetables. Garnish with more fresh rosemary or thyme sprigs if you like.

Serves 6

Mixed Grill, Juniper Aïoli

This is really perfect for a crowd when you are grilling outside. Folks could even grill their own. We cut the vegetables in a particular way to make them "grillable." We don't want them falling through the rack into the fire; we want a nice flat side, and we want them easy to grab and turn. The juniper aïoli has stood the test of time—still great with grilled meats and still requested after more than twenty years.

For the Juniper Aïoli

3 egg yolks
2 small potatoes, cooked and peeled, about ½ cup when puréed
15 juniper berries
3 cloves roasted garlic (see page 108)
1 teaspoon salt
Dash white pepper
⅓ cup white balsamic vinegar
2½ cups good-quality olive oil
½ cup fruity extra virgin olive oil

IN A FOOD PROCESSOR OR BLENDER, purée the egg yolks, potatoes, juniper berries, roasted garlic, salt, white pepper, and vinegar. When the mixture is absolutely smooth, pour in the oils in a slow, steady stream while the processor is running. Keep cold.

Makes 3 cups

Note: The aïoli will keep in the refrigerator for 1 week.

For the Grill (Per Serving)

1 cooked potato, split lengthwise

1 piece red bell pepper

1 piece pattypan squash, cut in half

1 wedge red onion

1 piece zucchini, split lengthwise

1 lamb chop

1 chicken sausage, such as Bruce Aidell's or other well-seasoned sausage,
*   cooked*

4 to 6 ounces of beef tenderloin, cut into chunks and skewered

Good-quality olive oil for brushing

Salt and freshly ground black pepper

LIGHT A MEDIUM-HOT FIRE IN A CHARCOAL GRILL, or preheat a gas grill. Brush the meats and vegetables with olive oil. Season with salt and pepper. Grill the vegetables first, then the lamb, sausage, and beef. The beef should cook fast—2 or 3 minutes. The lamb chop might take a little longer, depending on the thickness. Serve with the juniper aïoli for dipping.

Chef's Tip: If you soak the bamboo skewers in water for a couple of hours, they won't burn as easily on the grill.

Filet of Beef, Gorgonzola Sherry Cream, Horseradish Potatoes Gratin

The family Ascomyata is responsible for many foods we love. One form or another of the yeast spore is responsible for wine, beer, bread, and cheese. The spume and ferment of these bacteria create the great Bordeaux of France and the lowliest plonk. Yeast makes bread rise and beer foam. And bacteria give us cheeses. Oh, do I love mold! Gorgonzola dolce, Neal's Yard Cashel Blue, Point Reyes Blue, Bingham Hill, Oregon Blue, Morbier, Shropshire. Yum. This sauce uses a lowly domestic but is nonetheless quite tasty and has been a favorite at the restaurant for many years.

For the Potatoes

6 large Yukon Gold, russet, or other starchy potatoes
6 tablespoons unsalted butter, melted
2 tablespoons unbleached white flour
1 teaspoon salt
¼ teaspoon freshly ground black pepper
½ to ¾ cup prepared horseradish
¾ cup heavy cream
¾ cup grated Emmenthaler, Gruyère, Parmesan, or Gouda cheese,
*   or a combination of any or all of them*

PREHEAT THE OVEN TO 350°F. Scrub and peel the potatoes, slice them ⅛ to ¼ inch thick, and place in a bowl. Add the melted butter and flour and toss gently. Add the salt and pepper, then add the horseradish and the cream. Toss again.

LAYER THE POTATOES in an 8- by 12½- by 2-inch pan. Press them down, using the palm of your hand. Sprinkle the grated cheese over the top. Cover the entire pan with foil. Bake for 1 hour and

10 minutes. Remove the foil and continue baking for 20 minutes, or until the cheeses are bubbly and golden. Serve hot.

Note: Can be reheated at 250°F for 30 minutes.

For the Filets

Salt and freshly ground black pepper
6 center-cut Painted Hills filet mignons, each 1½ to 2 inches thick
Olive oil for brushing

SALT AND PEPPER THE FILETS on both sides and brush with olive oil. In a well-seasoned pan (see note below) sauté the steaks over high heat until a dark brown crust forms, about 3 minutes. Cook for 5 minutes per side for medium rare. Let steaks rest for 10 minutes in a warm place.

For the Gorgonzola Sherry Cream

½ cup red wine
4 to 6 cloves garlic, crushed
¼ cup sherry vinegar
½ cup good, unsalted beef stock
½ cup heavy cream
1 cup crumbled Gorgonzola cheese
¼ cup sherry

ADD THE WINE, GARLIC, AND SHERRY VINEGAR to the pan in which you sautéed the filets, and reduce to about 3 tablespoons. Add the beef stock and reduce to ½ cup. Add the cream. Reduce slightly, then whisk in Gorgonzola and sherry. Serve immediately with the filets and horse-radish potatoes gratin.

Serves 6

Chef's Tip: A seasoned pan is a steel or cast iron pan treated with oil. To season a pan, rub the inside with a generous amount of vegetable oil, lard, or bacon grease and place in a 250°F oven for 3 to 4 hours. Do not wash the pan. Wipe with a towel after each use. Reseason occasionally.

Pomegranate Lamb Chops, Rhubarb Mint Chutney

Rhubarb is best in the spring, before it gets tough and stringy in the sun. It arrives just about the same time as the Coffelts start butchering lambs. Now that we have an FDA-approved facility in the San Juans, I can legally serve island-raised grass-fed lamb and beef. I am so proud of our farmers and the food they raise. Sure, it's more expensive than those corporate products in the grocery, but it is really, truly worth it!

For the Rhubarb Mint Chutney

½ cup chopped dried apricots
2-inch piece ginger, peeled and finely minced
2 tablespoons chopped garlic
1½ cups cider vinegar
2 cups sugar
1 teaspoon whole mustard seeds
1 teaspoon ground cinnamon
¼ teaspoon crushed dried red chiles
6 cups chopped rhubarb
¾ cup chopped fresh mint

IN A NONREACTIVE POT, combine the apricots, ginger, garlic, vinegar, sugar, mustard seeds, cinnamon, and chiles, bring to a boil, and cook for 5 minutes or so. Add the rhubarb and continue cooking until the mixture returns to a boil, then lower the heat and stir, more or less constantly, for 15 minutes or so, until the chutney thickens. Remove from the heat and fold in the fresh mint. You can preserve the chutney in half-pint canning jars, following standard canning procedures, or keep it in a sealed container in the refrigerator for 8 days. The flavor improves over a few days.

Makes 3 to 4 cups

12 lamb rib chops
1 tablespoon finely minced garlic
1 tablespoon fresh oregano
Freshly ground black pepper
2 cups pomegranate juice

HAVE YOUR BUTCHER CUT the rib chops off the rack and trim the fat. Layer the chops in a nonreactive pan. Rub with the garlic and sprinkle oregano and pepper over each layer. Pour the pomegranate juice over the chops and allow to marinate in the refrigerator for at least 4 hours or overnight.

LIGHT A MEDIUM-HOT FIRE in a charcoal grill, or preheat a gas grill. Remove the chops from the marinade and grill for about 2 minutes per side for medium rare. Serve immediately with rhubarb mint chutney on the side.

Serves 4

Lamb and Morel Ragout, Shallots and Gold Beets

You don't have to use gold beets, but at Christina's we like them for the zap of color in what would otherwise be a very dark dish. We go through gallons of stock in the restaurant kitchen. It's a tough call, making stock. Our place isn't really big enough physically for us to make all the things we want. But in the summer we have 50 pounds of veal bones on the stove constantly, and we still can't make enough stock. Then there are the disasters, like the night I pulled the 5-gallon tub of beef stock from the refrigerator and promptly dropped it on the floor. If you like to cook but don't have the time to make stock, it's fine to buy some at the store. Lots of places sell perfectly good homemade stock: Roses Bakery in Eastsound and Pasta & Company in Seattle, for instance, and Dean & DeLuca in New York City. Even boxed stock from the grocery store can be made to work, though the canned stock is too salty.

Note: This is a braised stew; do not let it boil.

> *4 pounds lamb shoulder roast or leg, cut into large chunks*
> *Salt and freshly ground black pepper*
> *2 tablespoons good-quality olive oil*
> *½ cup cognac or brandy*
> *1 to 2 cups fresh morel mushrooms*
> *2 cups mushroom broth*
> *3 cups beef or lamb stock*
> *1 medium onion, cut into ¼-inch dice*
> *½ cup red wine*
> *1 teaspoon salt*
> *8 to 10 whole cloves garlic*
> *2 sprigs fresh thyme*

1 tablespoon dried marjoram
½ cup currant vinegar or other fruit vinegar
½ cup currant jelly or other seedless fruit jelly or jam
10 to 12 smallest fingerling or red potatoes
6 beets, preferably gold, cooked (see page 70), peeled, and cut into sixths
16 shallots, blanched (see page 15) and peeled
Freshly ground black pepper

PREHEAT THE OVEN TO 275°F. Salt and pepper the lamb pieces, then brown them in the olive oil over medium-high heat in a large Dutch oven or other heavy, oven-safe pot with a tight-fitting lid. Pour off the fat, add the cognac to the pot, and stir to deglaze.

IMMERSE THE MORELS in a saucepan of boiling water for 3 minutes. This step removes foreign matter and critters from the mushrooms. Drain the mushrooms and reserve the broth. Strain the broth through a fine-mesh sieve, China cap, cheesecloth, or other fine-mesh strainer.

ADD THE BROTH AND LAMB OR BEEF STOCK to the Dutch oven, then add the onion, red wine, and salt. Turn the heat to low and add the whole garlic cloves, thyme sprigs, marjoram, fruit vinegar, and currant jelly. Cover tightly and braise in the oven for 1½ hours. Remove from the oven and add the potatoes, beets, and shallots. Return to the oven and let braise for another 35 minutes.

REMOVE FROM THE OVEN and add the morel mushrooms. Return to the oven and braise for another 30 minutes or so. Add pepper to taste and serve in warmed bowls.

Serves 6 to 8

Rib-Eye Steak, Mushrooms, Alice Waters' Onion Rings

Among beef lovers there is plenty of discussion about the merits of various cuts of beef. My summers in the cookhouse at the Bar U Ranch were a culinary education I didn't even know I was getting. Beef was served every day. The big meal was at noon. This meant the roasts went in the oven by 9:30 or 10. The daily fare was usually pot roasts, short ribs, stew, heart, joints, shanks, and roasts. Anything ground was looked down on by the cowboys. No casseroles were allowed except as side dishes. Vegetables stewed to forever were good, except in summer, when everything out of the garden was eaten practically raw. Gravy was de rigueur, big vats of it. Pies for dessert were made fresh every morning, three or four of them. But what really made the cowboys on the benches sit up and take notice was rib-eye steak. There was a hint of reverence in the silence when Cook hefted that enormous platter of thick fried beefsteaks out from behind the stove. There was more laughter, it was gentler, softer, the teasing went to good-natured instead of bordering on mean, and it got real quiet. Until someone, maybe Einar or Red, neither of whom was afraid to speak up, said, "Damn, Ralph, that's good beef. Lookee, she cut like butter, don't need no steak knife." I would sit quiet and pleased, for I had spent the morning under Cook's direction carefully salting and peppering each steak on both sides.

Alice Waters, of Chez Panisse fame, came up with this exquisitely simple method for crispy, delectable onion rings.

For the Onion Rings

> *4 large yellow onions*
> *3 cups buttermilk*
> *Peanut oil for frying*
> *2 cups unbleached white flour*
> *Salt*
> *White pepper*

TRIM THE ENDS OFF THE ONIONS and slice into rings ½ to ¾ inch thick. Carefully remove the outer skin from the onions, then separate the rings. (Reserve the small ends and centers of the onions for another use.) Marinate the rings in the buttermilk for at least 1 hour. In a large, deep saucepan, heat 4 inches of peanut oil to 375°F. Then season the flour with salt and white pepper to taste, and dredge the rings in it until well coated. Fry the rings in the hot oil until crispy and golden, about 2 minutes, turning them once. Drain on paper towels before serving.

Salt and freshly ground black pepper
4 rib-eye or Spencer steaks
¼ cup cognac
2 shallots, finely chopped
2 tablespoons unsalted butter
3 cloves garlic, minced
1 pound mushrooms—chanterelles, morels, porcini, cremini, or
  portobellos
1 teaspoon fresh marjoram
1 tablespoon Dijon mustard
½ cup chopped flat-leaf Italian parsley

SALT AND LIGHTLY PEPPER BOTH SIDES OF EACH STEAK. In a well-seasoned pan, sear the steaks over high heat, browning well, about 4 minutes on each side for medium rare. Remove the steaks to a warm platter and let rest for 20 minutes before serving. Add the cognac and stir to deglaze the pan, and then add the shallots, butter, and garlic. Sauté for a minute and add the mushrooms. Cook for 3 minutes or so. Add the marjoram and mustard and stir to combine. Let rest in the pan over the lowest heat for 5 to 10 minutes, then add the parsley and toss. Add salt to taste.

To Serve

PLACE THE STEAKS ON A PLATTER or on individual plates, surround with the mushrooms, and top with the onion rings.

Serves 4

Braised Short Ribs, Spicy Sweet Potatoes

This is the kind of one-dish meal made easy by the electronic timers now available on most stoves. You braise the meat, put it in a pot with the other ingredients, and leave it in the refrigerator overnight. In the morning, the pot goes in the oven and you set the timer to turn the oven on three hours before you'll get home from work. The ribs won't be bothered by heating up along with the oven, and they will sit there happily for a couple of hours if you get caught in traffic. When you get home, there will be a vaguely spicy aroma in the air that will get everybody to the table on time.

2 tablespoons peanut oil
7 pounds beef short ribs
2 cups tomato juice
1 medium onion, chopped
4 cloves garlic, crushed
1 teaspoon ground cumin
½ teaspoon ground cloves
½ teaspoon cayenne (optional)
½ teaspoon ground allspice
1 tablespoon ground cinnamon
2 tablespoons sugar
2 tablespoons malt vinegar
Salt
Freshly ground black pepper
½ cup cold water
¼ cup unbleached white flour

PREHEAT THE OVEN TO 275°F. Heat the peanut oil in an oven-safe Dutch oven or large saucepan over medium-high heat. Brown the short ribs on all sides. In a medium saucepan, combine the tomato juice, onion, garlic, cumin, cloves, cayenne, allspice, cinnamon, sugar, vinegar, salt, and pepper, and bring to a boil. Pour over the browned ribs and braise in the oven for 3 hours, or until the meat is tender. Place the meat on a platter in a warm place.

MEASURE THE LIQUID IN THE PAN by pouring it into a measuring cup; add water or red wine, if necessary, to make 2 cups. Return the liquid to the pan. In a small bowl, blend the cold water with the flour to make a smooth paste. Bring the liquid in the pan to a boil, and gradually whisk in the paste. Whisk briskly until thickened, and remove from the heat. Pour the sauce over the short ribs and serve with the sweet potatoes (recipe follows).

For the Sweet Potatoes

> *5 large sweet potatoes*
> *Salt*
> *Peanut oil for sautéing*

COOK THE SWEET POTATOES WHOLE in boiling, salted water for about 20 minutes, or until tender. Chill.

Note: At this point they may be refrigerated for up to 3 days.

WHEN READY TO SERVE, peel the potatoes with a paring knife and cut into long wedges. In a large sauté pan over medium-high heat, add enough oil to cover the bottom of the pan. Sauté the potato wedges for about 2 minutes per side, until dark and crispy. Drain on paper towels and serve with the ribs and spicy sauce.

Serves 4 to 6

New York Steak, Tipsy Onion Butter, Fatso Mashed Potatoes

Sad to say, I have gained several pounds tasting these mashed potatoes. They have to be just right. I finally wised up and took them off the menu. Alas, the damage was done. The butter is a takeoff on the classic maitre d'hotel butter; the bourbon makes it so much better. All right, it's steak, butter, carbohydrates, and more butter. Yum. Just don't eat it every day.

For the Tipsy Onion Butter

1½ cups (3 sticks) unsalted butter, at room temperature
½ cup finely minced shallots
4 cloves garlic, mashed
1 tablespoon Bar U Ranch Mustard (see page 7) or other hot, sweet mustard
½ cup Jack Daniels or other bourbon
2 teaspoons fresh whole thyme leaves
2 teaspoons chopped fresh chervil
2 teaspoon chopped fresh parsley
Salt

PLACE THE SOFTENED BUTTER IN A BOWL and add the remaining ingredients. Mash together with a fork until all the ingredients are well blended. Form the butter into a log, wrap in plastic, and chill for at least 2 hours.

Makes about 2 cups

For the Mashed Potatoes

6 large Yellow Finn, Red Bliss, or other flavorful potatoes, peeled and cut
into sixths
12 cloves garlic, peeled
1 cup (2 sticks) unsalted butter
½ cup heavy cream
Salt
Fresh sage leaves for garnish

IN A LARGE SAUCEPAN, cook the potatoes and garlic in boiling salted water to cover for 15 to 20 minutes, until the potatoes are tender and a fork slides out easily. Drain off all the water. While the spuds and garlic are hot, add the butter and cream. Mash with a masher to a fare-thee-well. Add salt to taste. Keep in a warm place until ready to serve. Garnish with sage leaves just before serving.

Makes 6 to 8 servings

For the Steaks

4 New York steaks, 7 ounces each
Good-quality olive oil for brushing
Salt and freshly ground black pepper

IF YOU WILL BE GRILLING THE STEAKS, light a medium-hot fire in a charcoal grill, or preheat a gas grill. Brush the steaks on each side with olive oil. Salt and pepper to taste. Grill or pan-fry the steaks over high heat for 3 minutes per side for medium rare. Let the steaks rest for 10 minutes before serving. Top the steaks with a pat or two of the chilled onion butter. Serve with mashed potatoes.

Serves 4 generously

Sage-Roasted Chicken, Porcini Bread Pudding

At Christina's we bake several different breads for our basket everyday. I like having the baskets full on the table, whether people are eating bread or not. A celebratory meal in a restaurant is for me all about abundance, generosity of spirit, and sharing. Bread is a mark of a fine restaurant. It has to be fresh, good, bountiful, and provided no matter what is ordered. If all a customer orders is a bowl of soup and some bread, so be it. Let the bread keep coming. The other half of the equation is that we make it anyway—let's get it out there to those who want it. Consequently we always have lots of bread in the kitchen and this recipe works best with bread that is at least a day old. The recipe also satisfies other pet theories about adaptive reuse and resourceful living. Plus, it is a great way to get lots of profound and haunting porcini mushroom flavor without making a huge dent in your mushroom budget.

For the Bread Pudding

1½ cups chicken stock
2 ounces dried porcini mushrooms
4 cups cubed day-old bread
2 tablespoons chopped flat-leaf Italian parsley
2 teaspoons dried marjoram
1 teaspoon dried thyme
½ cup (1 stick) unsalted butter
1 small red onion, minced
2 cups sliced fresh chanterelle or porcini mushrooms
2 cloves garlic, minced
2 eggs, lightly beaten

IN A SMALL SAUCEPAN OVER MEDIUM HEAT, bring the stock just to a simmer. Remove from the heat and add the dried mushrooms. Set aside for 15 minutes.

MEANWHILE, IN A LARGE BOWL, toss the bread cubes with the parsley, marjoram, and thyme. Set aside. In a medium saucepan, melt the butter over medium heat. Add the onion and cook, stirring occasionally, for 5 minutes. Stir in the fresh mushrooms and garlic. Cook, stirring occasionally, until the mushrooms are soft, about 5 minutes. Add this mixture to the bread cubes, tossing gently.

DRAIN THE STOCK from the dried porcini mushrooms, reserving the liquid. Mince the mushrooms and add them to the bread mixture along with the reserved liquid. Fold well until the bread cubes are thoroughly moistened. Cover and let sit for 1 hour.

PREHEAT THE OVEN TO 350°F. Generously butter an 8½- by 4½-inch loaf pan. Add the eggs to the bread mixture; fold well. Place in the prepared pan, cover with a sheet of buttered foil, and bake in a *bain-marie* (see the Chef's Tip on page 57) until firm, about 1 hour. Let cool in the pan for 15 minutes.

TURN THE BREAD PUDDING OUT ONTO A BOARD and cut into thick slices. Serve warm with the roasted chicken.

For the Chicken

1 large fryer, cut into pieces
20 fresh sage leaves
Herbes de Provence (see page 6)
Salt and freshly ground black pepper
Unsalted butter, melted, for brushing

PREHEAT THE OVEN TO 400°F. Freeze the neck, back, and wings of the bird to use for stock. Carefully lift up the skin on the cut side of the breast and slide your fingers between the flesh and the skin, making sure the skin is still attached on at least one side. Insert whole sage leaves under the skin and pat the skin back in place. Repeat the procedure on the thighs and legs.

IN A LARGE BOWL, toss the chicken with the herbs and salt and pepper. Place the pieces of chicken in a shallow roasting pan and brush with melted butter.

ROAST IN THE OVEN FOR 40 MINUTES OR SO, until the juice from the leg runs clear. If necessary, make a small cut on the underside of a thigh to see if the meat is cooked through. Remove from the oven and serve immediately with slices of porcini bread pudding.

Serves 4

Chef's Tip: To get the best flavor out of dried herbs, rub them in the palm of your hand before adding, to break up the leaves and release the flavor.

Smoked Paprika Chicken, Corn Pudding

There are a million ways to cook chicken, but over the years I have distilled all my chicken cooking into one glorious method: the classic roast, of course. Roasted chicken done correctly is one of the great pleasures of the table: golden, crispy skin and moist, warm, tender shards of meat, simply accomplished by sticking a trussed bird in a hot oven for the right amount of time.

For the Corn Pudding

6 cups cooked corn kernels, scraped off the cob
1 cup heavy cream
½ cup (1 stick) unsalted butter
4 eggs
3 tablespoons sugar
1 cup bread crumbs
½ teaspoon white pepper
1 teaspoon salt

PREHEAT THE OVEN TO 350°F. In a food processor or blender, purée 3 cups of the corn with the cream. Melt the butter in a saucepan or in the microwave. In a medium bowl, combine the melted butter and the puréed corn. In a large bowl, beat the eggs, then add the corn mixture, sugar, bread crumbs, the remaining 3 cups whole kernels, white pepper, and salt. Fold the mixture into a buttered 3-quart casserole and bake in a *bain-marie* (see the Chef's Tip on page 57) for 1½ hours or so, until the pudding is golden brown on top and set.

1 large chicken (4 to 6 pounds)
1 tablespoon fresh thyme
1½ teaspoons freshly ground black pepper
1 tablespoon smoked paprika
1 teaspoon salt
1 tablespoon finely chopped fresh garlic
¼ cup good-quality olive oil

IN A LARGE, NONREACTIVE PAN, dust the chicken generously with the thyme, pepper, paprika, and salt. Toss with the fresh garlic and drizzle with the olive oil. Marinate for at least 1 hour or overnight.

PREHEAT THE OVEN TO 400°F. Place the chicken in a roasting pan. Roast the chicken in the oven for 45 minutes, or until the skin is crispy and golden, and the juices run clear. Serve with the corn pudding.

Serves 6 to 8

Chef's Tip: A trussed chicken is one that has had the legs tied together and the wings wrapped and held to the body with butcher's string. For spit roasting, trussing is essential. For pan roasting, it helps the bird cook evenly and stay moist.

Spring Vegetable Pot Pie

You can use almost any vegetables for this pot pie. It could just as well be a winter, fall, or summer dish. The flavor will change along with the color and texture, of course, but cooking with the seasons is satisfying. Besides, why spend your shopping day trying to find morels in the fall? Just use chanterelles instead. At La Varenne, the now defunct cooking school in Paris, the instructor told the class that once they could make puff pastry perfectly they could then go out and buy it. It's fun to make if you have the time; if not, the boxes of puff pastry in the freezer section of the grocery are perfectly fine.

For the Broth

1 medium red onion, finely minced
1 tablespoon chopped garlic
3 tablespoons good-quality olive oil
4 cups vegetable (or chicken) stock
1 tablespoon chopped fresh tarragon
1 teaspoon chopped fresh thyme leaves
1 teaspoon dried marjoram
½ cup white wine
⅓ cup sherry vinegar
1 tablespoon honey
2 tablespoons cornstarch
1 cup heavy cream
Salt

IN A LARGE POT OVER MEDIUM-HIGH HEAT, sauté the onion and garlic in the oil until soft and translucent. Add the stock, tarragon, thyme, and marjoram. Simmer over medium heat for about 15 minutes, until the flavors marry, then mix in the wine, sherry vinegar, and honey. Keep at a simmer.

IN A SMALL BOWL, mix the cornstarch with the heavy cream until smooth, then whisk into the bubbling stock mixture. As soon as the stock thickens, remove it from the heat. Add salt to taste.

For the Pot Pies

6 big leaves black kale or Swiss chard, cut into 1-inch pieces
18 asparagus spears, washed, peeled, and cut into 1-inch pieces
12 fresh morel mushrooms
12 baby carrots, peeled, trimmed, and blanched
12 green onions, cut into 1-inch pieces
12 whole cipollini onions, peeled and blanched
6 fingerling potatoes, steamed until tender, cut into 1-inch chunks
6 small Yukon Gold potatoes, steamed until tender, cut into 1-inch chunks
1 cup fresh shelled peas
½ cup chopped chives
½ cup chopped flat-leaf Italian parsley
2 sheets (8- by 4-inch) puff pastry

PREHEAT THE OVEN TO 400°F. In 6 individual ramekins or bowls holding at least 1 cup each, assemble the pies as follows. Into each ramekin place 1 leaf black kale, asparagus pieces equal to 3 spears, 2 morels, 2 carrots, 2 green onions, 2 cipollini onions, 1 fingerling potato, 1 Yukon gold potato, a spoonful of peas, and a sprinkling of chives and parsley. Ladle some of the hot broth over the vegetables. Cut 6 generous rounds of puff pastry, making them large enough to drape over the tops of the ramekins, and crimp around the edges to seal. Place the ramekins on a baking sheet and bake until the pastry puffs and is golden brown, about 25 minutes. Serve immediately.

BEFORE BAKING, you can cut a design in the pastry tops if you wish.

Note: In place of the ramekins you can also use a single soup tureen large enough to hold all the ingredients, covered by puff pastry.

Serves 6

Chef's Tip: You can substitute 1 ounce of dried morels if fresh morels are not available. Before using, soak them in 1 cup of boiling water until softened; drain.

Rabbit Stew, Sage Dumplings

When I can get it, rabbit becomes one of the most popular things on the menu. Browning the pieces of meat is an important step in making a braise or stew. It gives meat its flavor and adds color to the ragout. The seasoning is crucial to the flavor of any dish, especially a stew, and since the flavor of the seasonings changes over the course of the cooking time I like to season at the beginning, in the middle, and at the end. This method also adds to the dish's depth of flavor.

For the Dumplings

2 cups unbleached white flour
1¼ teaspoons baking powder
¾ teaspoon salt
2 tablespoons crumbled dried sage leaves
¼ cup (½ stick) unsalted butter
½ to ⅔ cup half-and-half

IN A MEDIUM BOWL, combine the flour, baking powder, salt, and sage. Using a pastry blender or two knives, cut the butter into the flour mixture until it resembles coarse crumbs. Add ½ cup half-and-half, using more as necessary to make a soft, pliable dough. Do not overwork the dough or the dumplings will be tough. Turn the dough out onto a floured board and roll out about ½ inch thick. Cut into 2-inch circles and drop onto the simmering stew. Simmer as directed in the stew recipe.

For the Rabbit Stew

Unbleached white flour for dredging
1 teaspoon paprika
1 tablespoon salt
½ teaspoon white pepper
2 pounds rabbit loin, boned and cut into 1-inch chunks

2 tablespoons unsalted butter
2 tablespoons peanut oil
½ cup brandy or cognac
8 shallots, peeled
5 cloves garlic
4 sprigs fresh tarragon, chopped, or 1 teaspoon whole dried tarragon
1 tablespoon whole dried marjoram
4 sprigs fresh thyme, or ½ teaspoon dried whole thyme
4 cups chicken stock
2 tablespoons Dijon mustard
Salt
2 tablespoons chopped flat-leaf Italian parsley

IN A WIDE, SHALLOW BOWL, blend the flour together with the paprika, salt, and white pepper, then toss the chunks of rabbit in the flour mixture until well coated.

IN A LARGE, FLAMEPROOF CASSEROLE, melt the butter with the peanut oil and brown the rabbit over medium heat, in batches if necessary. Remove the browned meat to a platter, add the brandy to the casserole, and stir to deglaze it.

CUT THE SHALLOTS IN HALF LENGTHWISE, leaving them joined by the white root at one end. Place the rabbit, shallots, garlic, half of the herbs, and the chicken stock in the casserole. Cover with a tight-fitting lid and simmer for 30 minutes over low heat, stirring occasionally. Remove the lid and whisk in the mustard, then add the rest of the herbs. Drop the dumpling rounds onto the hot liquid on top of the stew. Cover and continue simmering for 20 minutes, or until the dumplings are puffed and firm. Add salt to taste.

SERVE THE STEW with the dumplings on top, garnished with the parsley.

Serves 6

Chef's Tip: Any pot of water will boil faster with the lid on, watched or not. If you want to steam something, a tight-fitting lid is essential to create the moist, hot environment for the quick cook of steaming. If you don't want to lose any of your cooking liquids to evaporation, a lid is essential. In the process of braising, a lid or foil cover keeps the heat and the liquid in the pot, for the moist, slow cooking that is the essence of this technique.

Ravioli

BONNIE CARLOTTI WAS MY BEST FRIEND. HER MOTHER DROVE US ANY-
place we wanted to go in her big white Cadillac. My mother didn't drive.
After-school snacks were abundant at Bonnie's: cake, cookies, brownies,
a refrigerator full of Cokes and 7-UPs. Bonnie's father was a dentist. At
my house, my mother railed against the evils of tooth decay and had
apples for after school. Bonnie got one of the very first electric tooth-
brushes. My mother scoffed at such lazines. I spent quite a bit of time at
Bonnie's. WHEN BONNIE'S GRANDMOTHER VISITED from Italy, I
was informed that there would be no sleepovers because she would be
staying in Bonnie's toy-crammed room. My own grandmother was an
elegant cowgirl, college educated, who smoked, drank scotch by the tum-
bler, and made considered remarks that brought gales of laughter from
the adults. Bonnie's Nana from Italy was a revelation. She was shorter
than I was, wore all black, didn't speak a word of English, and was always
in the kitchen. I loved her. In my small Oregon town of the fifties, she
was the most exotic personage ever. Bonnie was embarrassed when she
explained to me that her Nana would be taking over the kitchen, and
the supply of treats might come to an end. But Nana did other things
that were fun to watch, and I could still come to lunch. ONE DAY
WE SAT DOWN TO BOWLS of something called "minestrone." Dr. Carlotti
was almost weeping with pleasure as he showed me how to grate the

cheese over the top. Bonnie chose to have Campbell's chicken noodle soup. I couldn't believe soup could be so good. The good doctor told me that if I liked the minestrone I could come again for lunch tomorrow: Mama would be making ravioli. Did I know what ravioli was? Of course I didn't. The soup was great, but the ravioli turned out to be something divine. We ate and ate. Nana filled the big bowls time after time. Bonnie's mother watched with apprehension. I had yet to learn that a hearty appetite was considered unladylike by some. It was ten years before I saw ravioli again, and then it was an enormous disappointment. The clumsy slabs of noodle filled with hamburger and covered with a sharp tomato sauce were nothing like the delicate pillows of flavor I remembered.

Three Raviolis

I offer here three fillings for ravioli. Each is fairly easy to make and can be made in large batches and kept ready in the freezer for consoling the lovesick, for feeding that returned someone you hoped never to see again, or for those moments of total despair. The little Atlas Pasta Maker is an indispensable kitchen tool: turn the crank and out roll smooth, flat, thin sheets of satiny dough just ready and willing for you to have your way with them. Freeze the ravioli on flat sheet pans lined with parchment paper. After they are firm, place them in *labeled* freezer bags. To thaw, remove the ravioli from the freezer bag and separate them on a parchment-lined sheet pan. Then return them to the refrigerator to thaw completely.

For the Pasta

1 cup semolina flour
3 cups unbleached white flour
½ teaspoon salt
4 large eggs
1 tablespoon water, if necessary

MIX THE SEMOLINA AND WHITE FLOURS and salt in a pile on your work surface. Make a well in the middle and add the eggs and just enough of the water to work the dough into a soft, pliable mass. Knead the dough for 10 minutes, until smooth and satiny.

THE DOUGH CAN ALSO BE MIXED in a food processor by adding the eggs to the flour mixture and pulsing a few times or so, until the dough is dry and crumbly. Turn the dough out onto the board and knead until smooth and satiny.

WRAP THE DOUGH IN PLASTIC and let it rest in the refrigerator for 1 hour.

CUT THE DOUGH INTO 3 PIECES and, using an Atlas or other hand-cranked pasta roller, begin by running the dough through the number 1 (widest) setting. This will be difficult the first couple of times you roll it through. Just keep putting the dough through the machine until the sheet of dough is workable. Gradually increase the numbers to roll the pasta sheet thinner and thinner. Work up to 7 on the dial, at which point the sheet of pasta will be very long and very thin. It may be cut into shorter pieces if counter space is at a premium.

BRUSH OR SPRAY THE RECTANGLE OF DOUGH with a little water and dot one side of the pasta sheet with a hefty tablespoon of the filling (recipes follow) every ¾ inch or so. Fold the dough over the row of filling and press between the mounds of filling to seal the dough. Cut with a knife or a little rolling cutter to form the squares of ravioli. If you won't be cooking the ravioli within a few hours, they freeze very well.

Serves 6 very generously

Sweet Potato and Leek Filling

>*1 large sweet potato, cooked and peeled*
>*5 cloves garlic, finely minced*
>*1 large leek, split, washed, and cut into ¼-inch dice*
>*2 tablespoons good-quality olive oil*
>*½ teaspoon salt*
>*1 cup grated Romano cheese*

WASH THE SWEET POTATO IN A BOWL and set aside. In a sauté pan, brown the garlic and leek in the oil and pour over the sweet potato. While still hot, mash the mixture together, then add the salt and cheese. Chill until ready to use.

Swiss Chard and Ricotta Filling

2 cups ricotta cheese
1 bunch Swiss chard
½ cup chopped pancetta
5 cloves garlic, chopped
1 tablespoon sherry vinegar
1 cup grated Parmigiano-Reggiano cheese

PURÉE THE RICOTTA IN A FOOD PROCESSOR or mash it through a fine-mesh sieve to make it smooth. Trim the Swiss chard and discard the largest part of the stems. Chop the chard into ½-inch dice. Sauté the pancetta in a large pan over high heat; add the chopped garlic cloves just as the pancetta begins to brown. The pancetta will release enough fat to oil the pan. Continue until the pancetta is crispy and the garlic has begun to caramelize. Add the chopped chard and sauté for 3 minutes more, until the chard is wilted, soft, and bright green. Remove from the heat and add the vinegar to the chard. Combine the chard with the ricotta and grated Parmesan and mix well. Chill for 1 hour before using.

Dungeness Crab Filling

¾ cup ricotta cheese
1 pound cooked Dungeness crabmeat
½ cup chopped Italian flat-leaf parsley
⅓ cup chopped chives

PURÉE THE RICOTTA IN A FOOD PROCESSOR or mash it through a fine-mesh sieve to make it smooth. Mix with the remaining ingredients in a large bowl. Chill for 1 hour before using.

To Cook the Ravioli

DROP THE RAVIOLI INTO RAPIDLY BOILING salted water and cook for 2 minutes (5 minutes, if cooking frozen ravioli), or until the ravioli are tender and toothsome or al dente, just barely offering resistance to the tooth. Drain and serve immediately.

Chef's Tip: Rather than bury the flavor of the ravioli under a heavy tomato sauce, I prefer to toss the ravioli with herbed chicken stock. In a medium-sized pot, heat a cup or so of chicken stock with 2 or 3 tablespoons of chopped fresh herbs like chives, marjoram, basil, parsley, and lemon zest. Any combination will do. Heat the stock slowly for 10 minutes or so, just enough to infuse their flavor without cooking the life out of the herbs. Sprinkle with more fresh herbs just before serving.

Roast Pheasant, Pumpkin Risotto, Black Walnut Gremolata

Pheasants these days are farm-raised, plump, and available year-round. Nonetheless, to me they are a fall and winter food, mostly because I spent several Thanksgivings and Sundays in December sitting in the back of a cold bunkhouse plucking birds, surrounded by the stink of burning feathers. Imagine, then, the delicate, fine-textured flesh—lean, richly flavored, and seasoned—served by candlelight at a soothing, languid pace in a small restaurant with the face you love across the table and a bottle of fine old Burgundy between you.

For the Pheasants

Salt and freshly ground black pepper
2 whole pheasants, 4 to 6 pounds each
Good-quality olive oil for basting

PREHEAT THE OVEN TO 350°F. Salt and pepper the birds well, inside and out, and truss them by wrapping them with string as you would wrap packages, making sure to tie the wing tips and drumsticks to the body. At this point, you can skewer the pheasants with the rods provided with your oven rotisserie or place them on a rack in a pan deep enough to catch the basting oil. Brush with olive oil and roast in the oven for 40 minutes, until either the leg joint is loose and the juices run clear or a meat thermometer inserted into the thickest part of the leg reads 185°F. Let the birds rest for 20 minutes or so before carving.

For the Risotto

½ cup finely chopped red onion
1 tablespoon finely chopped garlic
3 tablespoons unsalted butter
2 cups arborio rice
4 to 5 cups chicken stock

1 cup cooked, mashed pumpkin
1 tablespoon crumbled dried sage leaves
1 tablespoon crumbled dried marjoram leaves
Salt
½ cup grated Asiago cheese

IN A LARGE POT, sauté the onion and garlic in the butter until soft and translucent. Add the rice and enough of the stock to almost cover the rice. Reduce the heat to medium and stir the rice until it absorbs the stock. Keep on stirring and cooking the rice, adding more stock as it is absorbed. After you have used half the stock, add the pumpkin, sage, and marjoram. Stir and keep on cooking over medium heat until all the stock is absorbed and the rice is tender but toothsome. The risotto should not be soupy or too liquid, but neither should it be dry; it should be somewhere in between. Add salt to taste. Fold in the Asiago and serve warm.

For the Gremolata

¼ cup black walnut pieces
¼ cup chopped Italian flat-leaf parsley
¼ cup very finely minced garlic
2 tablespoons finely chopped fresh thyme
Grated zest of 2 lemons

PREHEAT THE OVEN TO 400°F. Place the black walnut pieces in a small pan and toast in the oven for 3 minutes or so. Finely chop the nuts, then toss in a bowl with the remaining ingredients.

Makes about 6 tablespoons

To Serve

CUT THE COOKED PHEASANTS INTO PIECES and serve on individual plates with the risotto. Pass the gremolata.

Serves 6

Desserts

Steamed Persimmon Pudding

Apple Fritters, Buttermilk Ice Cream

Mile-High Coconut Cake

Real Strawberry Shortcake

Rhubarb Buckle, Ginger Ice Cream

Cappuccino Cheesecake

Peach Ice Cream, Almond Shortbread

Plum Cake, Brandy Cream Filling

Wild Blackberry Crema

Gooseberry Fool, Coconut Tuiles

Lavender Ice Cream, Hungarian Butterhorns

Chocolate Blackout Torte

Chocolate Pavé

Poached Cherries

Doug Fir Granita

Three Ices: Currant, Blood Orange Maple, and Chocolate

Raspberry Trifle Torte

Wild Blackberry Crema, page 224

Steamed Persimmon Pudding

I saw my first persimmon in Geneva. In my room on the seventh floor, the crimson-orange fruit wrapped in purple tissue was a jewel on my tin breakfast trolley. At first I thought it was a tomato, but as I pulled back the delicate paper (what a sumptuous rustle it made), I could tell by the stem, really the calyx, that it was something very different. The persimmon was very soft, and it smelled vaguely like a garden. I took a bite. It tasted like a flower and a lemon, with a faintly sweet finish. The juice ran down my chin. After the food revolution in the eighties, persimmons started appearing at our Island Market. Do not bite into a hard, unripe persimmon; they are so dry and sour that your tongue could be damaged. Let them sit on the windowsill for a few days until they soften.

3 cups unbleached white flour
½ cup (1 stick) unsalted butter, at room temperature
1½ cups sugar
2 eggs
2 tablespoons maple syrup
2 large, ripe persimmons
2 tablespoons Pickled Ginger (see page 17)
1 cup dried cranberries
1 cup golden raisins
1 teaspoon ground cinnamon
⅛ teaspoon ground mace
1 teaspoon ground nutmeg
1 tablespoon Drambuie
1 tablespoon vanilla extract

IN A LARGE BOWL, blend the flour and butter. Add the sugar, eggs, and maple syrup. Cut the persimmons in half and scoop the ripe flesh away from the skin. Purée the persimmon flesh with the Pickled Ginger in a food processor or blender, then blend this mixture into the batter. Fold in the dried cranberries, raisins, spices, Drambuie, and vanilla. Steam over boiling water in a buttered 1 quart mold for 2 hours, or until a toothpick inserted in the middle comes out clean. Cool for 2 hours before unmolding. Slice and serve with a little sweetened whipped cream.

Serves 6 to 8

Apple Fritters, Buttermilk Ice Cream

My grandmother made her own doughnuts. There were no doughnut shops in eastern Washington. Doughnuts have gotten a bad rap, but they are certainly no more dangerous than a French fry. If you have never eaten a fresh homemade doughnut, you should, at least once in your life. Do not count the airy, tasteless, too-sweet numbers from those popular franchises.

We make these apple fritters to order at the restaurant, but only in the winter, when we're not so busy. If the oil is hot enough, the fritters will absorb a minimum of fat and stay crisp on the outside while the apple remains toothsome and sweet.

For the Fritters

2½ cups unbleached white flour
2 teaspoons baking powder
½ cup sugar
2 eggs
½ cup heavy cream
1 teaspoon vanilla extract
1 drop lemon extract
5 large, firm apples, such as Braeburn or Gravenstein
4 cups peanut oil for frying
Powdered sugar for dusting

IN A WIDE, SHALLOW BOWL, blend the flour, baking powder, and sugar together, then whisk in the eggs, cream, vanilla extract, and lemon extract. Peel and core the apples then cut them into rings. Dip the apple slices in the batter; each slice should be covered with a thin layer of batter.

IN A LARGE, DEEP SAUCEPAN, heat the peanut oil to 365°F. Fry the batter-coated apple slices in batches for 2 to 3 minutes, turning them once, until they are golden brown and crispy. Drain on paper towels and dust with the powdered sugar. Serve warm with a scoop of buttermilk ice cream (recipe follows).

Serves 6 to 8

For the Ice Cream

3 cups heavy cream
6 egg yolks
2 cups sugar
2 cups buttermilk
1 vanilla bean, scraped

MIX 1 CUP OF THE CREAM with the egg yolks and cook in a double boiler over hot water until creamy. In a bowl, combine the remaining 2 cups cream, sugar, buttermilk, and the seeds from the vanilla bean. Add the hot cream mixture and whisk well. Chill. Freeze in an ice cream maker according to the manufacturer's directions.

Makes about 1½ quarts

Mile-High Coconut Cake

There is nothing like a big fluffy cake to set my heart racing. My mother carefully sorted our Halloween candy, removing the bubble gum and anything else she thought necessary to save us from the dreaded tooth decay. We didn't have Cokes in our refrigerator, and we didn't have a cookie jar. Sweets were considered some kind of weakness. Birthday cakes were intermittent until my father wised up and started bringing them home from a bakery. Otherwise, I learned young that if I wanted cake I would have to bake it myself.

Putting a cake together can be daunting if you haven't done it before, but it's really not difficult. Just jump in and give it a try. For a cake with many layers, it's a good idea to frost between the layers first and let it chill in the refrigerator for a few hours before you tackle frosting the outside. This is an easy cake and results in lots of oohs and ahs.

For the Cake

1½ sticks unsalted butter, at room temperature
1¾ cups sugar
4 eggs, separated
1 tablespoon vanilla extract
Grated zest of 1 lemon
3 cups sifted cake flour
1½ cups milk
2 teaspoons baking powder

PREHEAT THE OVEN TO 375°F. In a large bowl, using an electric mixer, whip the softened butter at medium speed; add the sugar and continue beating until the mixture is light and fluffy. Beat in the egg yolks, vanilla extract, and lemon zest. On low speed, add 1 cup of the flour and ½ cup of the milk. Add the baking powder. Continue mixing and alternately adding the remaining 2 cups flour and 1 cup milk until they

are completely incorporated and the batter is smooth and creamy. Set aside.

IN A MEDIUM BOWL, whip the egg whites until soft peaks form. Fold into the batter, taking care not to deflate the whites.

BUTTER AND FLOUR three 8-inch cake pans. Divide the batter among the pans. Bake for 30 minutes or so, until the top of the cake bounces back when touched and a toothpick inserted into the cake comes out clean. Cool in the pans for 10 minutes, and then turn the cakes out onto a rack or parchment to finish cooling.

For the Filling

1 cup sugar
1 can (13.5 ounces) coconut milk
2 drops coconut extract
3 egg whites, at room temperature
1½ cups (3 sticks) unsalted butter, cut into small pieces

IN A MEDIUM SAUCEPAN, heat the sugar, coconut milk, and coconut extract together over high heat. In a large mixing bowl, using an electric mixer, whip the egg whites until soft peaks form. Cook the sugar mixture until it is bubbling and the sugar is dissolved. With the mixer running, pour the sugar mixture into the egg whites and continue beating until stiff peaks form and the meringue is shiny. Continue beating to cool the mixture a little. Add the butter, bit by bit, and continue beating until the buttercream forms. Set aside.

SPLIT THE COOLED CAKE LAYERS IN HALF and fill between the layers with the buttercream. Stack and fill all the layers and refrigerate for an hour or so to allow the filling to set.

For the Icing

4 egg whites, at room temperature
1½ cups sugar
⅓ cup light corn syrup
⅓ cup water
1 teaspoon vanilla extract
8 ounces shredded, sweetened coconut

IN A LARGE MIXING BOWL, using an electric mixer, whip the egg whites until stiff peaks form. In a medium saucepan, bring the sugar, corn syrup, and water to a boil and cook until the mixture is clear and a second syrup has formed, about 2 minutes. With the mixer on high speed, pour the syrup into the beaten egg whites and keep beating until stiff peaks form and the meringue is glossy. Add the vanilla and beat a few seconds more until it is completely incorporated.

IT IS IMPORTANT to use the icing immediately, as it sets up rapidly. Ice the cake generously on the top and sides. After the cake is covered with icing, shower it with shredded coconut and use a spatula to press the coconut onto the sides, taking care to cover the icing completely. Covered, this cake keeps for 4 days.

Serves 12 to 14

Real Strawberry Shortcake

This is the dessert my mother *did* make at home. During strawberry season, I would arrive home from school to find the breezeway stacked with flats of strawberries. It would have been with some vigor that I hit the kickstand on my bike, knowing that I would be spending the next several hours washing and hulling berries for one of my mom's preserving projects. Great training for a chef, it turns out. When the jars of jam were finished, I would set aside a few pints of especially big and juicy berries for dessert. Just as we sat down for dinner, Mom would put the shortcake in the oven, and just about the time we finished dinner it would be ready. It kept us all at the table. We never had whipped cream; instead, we just poured cream into our bowls.

Note: The method for cutting the berries in the bowl is a crucial part of this recipe. Not one drop of strawberry juice should escape.

For the Shortcake

2 cups unbleached white flour
2 teaspoons baking powder
½ teaspoon salt
2 tablespoons sugar
6 tablespoons unsalted butter
¾ cup heavy cream
Unsalted butter, melted, for brushing

PREHEAT THE OVEN TO 400°F. In a bowl, combine the flour, baking powder, salt, and sugar, and cut in the butter until it resembles coarse crumbs, or process the butter with the dry ingredients in a food processor. Gently beat in the cream until a dough forms.

DIVIDE THE DOUGH INTO 2 PIECES. In a buttered 8-inch cake pan, pat out one piece of the dough (¼ to ½ inch thick). Brush with melted butter. Repeat the procedure with the other piece of dough and place on top of the first piece of dough.

BAKE FOR 15 MINUTES, or until pale gold. Remove from the oven and let cool for at least 5 minutes.

For the Strawberries

4 pints berries
¾ to 1½ cups sugar

WASH AND HULL THE BERRIES CAREFULLY. Place 3 pints of the strawberries in a large bowl and add the sugar to taste. Using 2 table knives, cut across the berries in rows. Turn the bowl 90 degrees and cut the berries across the width of the bowl again. Let sit to macerate for at least 20 minutes. The berries will make their own fabulous juice. They will not keep longer than 5 hours. Reserve the remaining pint of whole berries for serving.

For the Chantilly Cream

2 cups heavy cream
½ cup powdered sugar
¼ cup Cointreau

USING AN ELECTRIC MIXER, beat the cream, sugar, and Cointreau in a large bowl at high speed, or whisk by hand, until stiff peaks form. If whisking by hand, use a chilled bowl, and make sure the cream is extra-cold; whisk for about 10 minutes.

To Serve

CUT SHORTCAKE INTO WEDGES. The butter between the layers will make them easy to split in half. Ladle berries onto the bottom piece of shortcake and top with the second piece. Pass the chantilly cream and reserved berries.

Serves 6 to 8

Desserts

WE DROVE THROUGH THE VILLAGE OF ROLLE, MY OLD STOMPING ground in the early seventies. It was unchanged, and was just a few miles down the road from my new destination, Fredy Girardet in Crissier, on the outskirts of Lausanne. Switzerland, the most sophisticated country in the world, was home to the world's greatest restaurant. We had arranged for our lunch months before and entered the small foyer in a mist of anticipation. At the table, the four of us pored over the menu, each determined to order three courses, none of them the same. After the champagne, the first courses started to arrive, and we got quiet and dug in. It was a sublime afternoon. The most memorable part of the meal for me was getting a piece of lobster shell in my bisque. It was a message from the universe about being a driven perfectionist. Even the great Fredy can end up serving a piece of lobster shell. ▨ THE DESSERT MENU WAS HUGE with a multitude of choices. As my piece of *gâteau marjolaine* was being placed in front of me, I noticed a trolley being wheeled to a table in the corner of the room. With a vague air of confusion, I watched the group of six poker-faced Japanese as they pointed to the various canisters of ice cream and sorbet. I forgot it, though, when my knife splintered through the layer of crusty meringue into the bed of dark chocolate mousse. ▨ IT WAS ONLY AFTER the dessert plates were removed and our coffee was brought that I began to pout. Why weren't we offered the ice cream trolley? I wondered. **⏸** THE CHECK ARRIVED. We were prepared. We had made a special trip to the bank in Lausanne to get some cash—Chef Girardet didn't take Visa. Then, when the trolley appeared at our table after we had paid, it all became clear to me. **⏸** TWO LEVELS OF FROSTY CANISTERS on a pewter cart, with a steward, all in white, rattling off the ice cream and sorbet choices. You could have one flavor, two . . . or all seventeen. Everything from chocolate, raspberry, and vanilla to chestnut, passion fruit, cognac, and holly berry. Naturally, we were all so well fed that it was impossible to eat much more, but the civilized nature of the excess and the ceremony that accompanied it made it de rigueur to have just a taste. We couldn't afford to sleep in Switzerland, so with full bellies, *El Permanente* drove us over the Alps to Lake Maggiore.

Rhubarb Buckle, Ginger Ice Cream

Every old farmhouse on the island used to have a patch of rhubarb growing somewhere around the back door. Chives, parsley, and mint dot the landscape as well, and these sturdy perennials continue to grow even after years of neglect. Fresh fruit and herbs have always been a part of country living.

Rhubarb in early spring is bright red and tender. The long, fibrous stems come later when the plant gets older and is exposed to more sun. Look for stems that are bright, short, and fat. Trim the ends and make sure all the leaf is removed. Rhubarb needs sugar to bring out its flavor; and ginger, in spite of its exotic origin, makes a natural pairing.

For the Ice Cream

2 cups heavy cream
1¾ cups sugar
6 eggs
3 tablespoons Pickled Ginger (see page 17)
4 cups half-and-half
1 teaspoon vanilla extract

HEAT 1 CUP OF THE HEAVY CREAM and the sugar in a saucepan until it is very hot and steaming but not boiling. In a bowl, whisk the eggs together well. Pour the hot cream mixture over the eggs, whisking well. When the cream is fully incorporated, pour the cream-and-egg mixture back into the saucepan and whisk over high heat for 3 minutes or so, until the mixture just begins to thicken. Remove from the heat and whisk in the remaining cream.

PURÉE THE PICKLED GINGER in a food processor or blender. In a large bowl, combine the custard mixture, puréed ginger, half-and-half, and vanilla. Whisk well and strain through a China cap or other fine-mesh strainer. Freeze in an ice cream maker according to the manufacturer's instructions.

Makes about 1½ quarts

For the Rhubarb Mix

> *8 cups fresh rhubarb, cut into 1- to 1½-inch chunks*
> *2½ to 3½ cups sugar*
> *½ cup ginger ale*
> *½ cup cornstarch*
> *1 tablespoon peeled, grated ginger*

PREHEAT THE OVEN TO 350°F. Toss the rhubarb, sugar, ginger ale, cornstarch, and ginger together in a large bowl, moistening all ingredients and making sure the cornstarch is dissolved. Place in a buttered 8- by 11-inch baking pan.

For the Topping

> *1 cup firmly packed brown sugar*
> *1 cup oatmeal*
> *½ cup unbleached white flour*
> *¾ cup (1½ sticks) unsalted butter, at room temperature*
> *1 teaspoon ground cinnamon*
> *1 teaspoon ground cardamom*
> *½ teaspoon ground cloves*

BLEND ALL OF THE INGREDIENTS TOGETHER in a bowl. Spoon over the rhubarb mixture, completely covering it.

BAKE FOR 1 HOUR AND 10 MINUTES, or until the topping is golden and the edges are quite bubbly. Serve in bowls with ginger ice cream.

Serves 10 to 12

Cappuccino Cheesecake

In the early eighties, when I was struggling to find desserts that I considered truly regional, cappuccino cheesecake was one I came up with. The week before I opened Christina's I had yet to find an espresso machine I could afford. I was convinced that my restaurant was not complete without an espresso machine. Everything I wanted to say about the goals and style of my place would start with the statement that an espresso machine made. Realizing I was not buying the $6,000 Maserati of espresso machines, Barbara, at Visions in Seattle, found an old single-group Gaggia in pretty good working condition. I was thrilled and immediately called my mother and begged her for one more loan of $1,500. In 1980, justifying this purchase to any banker would have been absurd. My mother just threw up her hands and wrote the check. It was the single most expensive thing I bought for the restaurant. We happily pulled thousands of espressos out of that machine until the boiler finally gave up the ghost in 1991. I loved that machine so much I made it into a coffee table. Oops, I mean a *cappuccino* table.

For the Chocolate Cookie Crust

> *1 package (9 ounces) chocolate wafer cookies*
> *½ cup sugar*
> *1 teaspoon ground cinnamon*
> *1 tablespoon unbleached white flour*
> *½ cup (1 stick) unsalted butter, melted*

PREHEAT THE OVEN TO 375°F. LACE the chocolate cookies in a food processor or blender and grind until they become fine crumbs. Add the sugar, cinnamon, and flour and combine thoroughly. Add the butter and pulse once or twice to mix. Turn the crumb mixture out into a 10-inch springform pan, and pat it down firmly to cover the bottom of the pan. Chill the crust for at least 10 minutes.

For the Topping

> ¾ cup sour cream
> 2 tablespoons sugar
> 2 tablespoons Kahlúa or other coffee liqueur

WHISK TOGETHER THE INGREDIENTS in a bowl and reserve.

For the Filling

> 2 pounds cream cheese, at room temperature
> 2 cups sugar
> 1 tablespoon unbleached white flour
> 1 teaspoon vanilla
> 4 large eggs
> ¼ cup double espresso
> 1 tablespoon Kahlúa or other coffee liqueur

IN A LARGE MIXING BOWL, using an electric mixer, beat the cream cheese with the sugar until the mixture is smooth and silky. Add the flour and vanilla, mixing well. Beat in the eggs, one at a time, mixing thoroughly after each addition. Spoon a third of the cream cheese mixture into a separate mixing bowl and whisk in the espresso and Kahlúa. Spoon half of the plain cream cheese mixture into a springform pan with a spatula. Top with the espresso mixture, then cover with the remaining plain cream cheese mixture. Tap the pan gently on the counter to settle the filling. Wrap the outside of the pan in foil and place it in a large roasting pan filled with enough warm water to come 2 inches up the sides of the springform pan (a *bain-marie*). Bake for 1½ hours.

REMOVE THE CHEESECAKE FROM THE OVEN and spread the sour cream mixture over the top. Return the pan to the oven, turn off the oven, and leave the cheesecake in the oven, with the door ajar, for at least 1½ hours. Chill thoroughly before removing the side of the pan and slicing. It will keep, refrigerated, for 6 days.

Serves 10 to 12

Peach Ice Cream, Almond Shortbread

For this ice cream you will need some really ripe peaches. I can always find them at Sosio's in the Pike Place Market in Seattle when they are noplace else. Ripe peaches are a sublime pleasure, and turning them into ice cream is a way to hold on to the pleasures of summer. George Orser here on the island grows beautiful tree-ripened peaches, and also Suze at Sosio's will be happy to send you some if it's been awhile since you tasted one. If you are young, you may not understand what the deal is with peaches, but that's because you have never eaten the real thing.

> *2 cups heavy cream*
> *2 cups sugar*
> *Seeds scraped from 1 vanilla bean (see the Chef's Tip on page 225)*
> *1 tablespoon unbleached white flour*
> *8 egg yolks*
> *5 cups half-and-half*
> *6 peaches, blanched and peeled*
> *1 teaspoon almond extract*
> *Almond Shortbread (see page 26)*

IN A MEDIUM SAUCEPAN, heat 1 cup of the cream with 1 cup of the sugar and add the vanilla seeds. Heat over high heat, whisking continuously, until the cream is steamy and hot. In a medium bowl, add the flour to the egg yolks and whisk until they are pale and foamy, about 3 minutes. Still whisking, add the hot cream mixture. Combine well, return to the saucepan, and cook, whisking, for 2 minutes more, until the mixture thickens. Remove from the heat and immediately add the remaining 1 cup cream and the half-and-half. Whisk together and refrigerate until ready to use.

CUT THE PEACHES FROM THEIR PITS into loose chunks, place in a large bowl, and add the remaining 1 cup sugar and the almond extract; let macerate for at least 1 hour. The peaches should absorb some of the sugar. This step will keep them somewhat soft even though frozen. After an hour or so, add the cream mixture to the peaches. Freeze in an ice cream maker according to the manufacturer's instructions. Serve with Almond Shortbread.

Makes almost 2 quarts

Plum Cake, Brandy Cream Filling

The Italian plum grows extremely well in the San Juan Islands. On Orcas, there are many old trees that produce an abundance of these lovely little dark purple plums with the delicate frosted skin. The flesh is golden yellow, juicy, and sweet. The season is short for these Italian plums. So preserving them by drying is the time-honored way of keeping this stone fruit available year-round.

1½ cups sugar
1 teaspoon salt
1 teaspoon ground nutmeg
1 teaspoon ground cinnamon
1 teaspoon ground ginger
1 teaspoon baking soda
2 cups unbleached white flour
3 eggs
1 cup peanut oil
1 cup buttermilk
1 cup dried plums, cut into ¼-inch dice
½ cup coarsely chopped shelled walnuts or hazelnuts (optional)

PREHEAT THE OVEN TO 300°F. In a medium bowl, combine the sugar, salt, nutmeg, cinnamon, ginger, baking soda, and flour, and set aside. In another, larger bowl, beat the eggs until pale yellow, then add the peanut oil and buttermilk. Mix in the dried plums and nuts. Gradually add the flour mixture to the egg mixture and mix well. Pour the batter into a buttered 8- by 8-inch baking pan and bake for 1 hour, or until a tester inserted in the middle of the cake comes out clean.

Brandy Cream Filling

1½ cups heavy cream
1 cup sugar
2 drops vanilla extract
1½ teaspoons gelatin
3 egg yolks
¾ cup brandy
½ cup (1 stick) unsalted butter, at room temperature, cut into chunks

COMBINE THE CREAM, SUGAR, VANILLA EXTRACT, and gelatin in a medium saucepan. Heat over medium heat until the mixture is steamy and hot but not boiling. In a large bowl, whisk the egg yolks; pour the hot cream mixture over the yolks while whisking. Return to the saucepan and cook over medium heat, whisking constantly, until the mixture thickens. Remove from the heat, add the brandy, and let cool for 10 minutes. Whisk in the softened butter and chill. Refrigerate until ready to use.

Makes about 1½ cups

To Serve

LET THE CAKE COOL FOR AN HOUR. Split the layer by cutting horizontally and fill with the chilled brandy cream. Return the cake to the refrigerator for at least an hour before serving. The cake will keep, refrigerated for 3 days.

Serves 8 to 10

Chef's Tip: To oven-dry Italian plums, split them in half lengthwise and remove the pit. Place skin side down on a sheet of baking parchment or foil. Place in 200°F oven for 10 to 12 hours or overnight.

Apples

AFTER THE EASILY ACCESSIBLE CEDARS AND FIRS WERE HARVESTED, the San Juan Islands were a sea of hillside stumps. Imagine the work it took to remove trees with a team of horses and a rope. That is what the island homesteaders were faced with when they decided to plant orchards. These orchards became the first local wealth. By the turn of the century, the islands were the premier fruit-growing region in the state, and the apples and pears from Westsound and Crow Valley were prizewinners at the state fair and commanded top dollar at the markets in Seattle. Strawberries, for instance, traveled by steamer from Olga to Bellingham, then by train to Montana and points beyond. THERE WERE SOME GOOD YEARS before the orchards of Hood River, with its plentiful water, outpaced the islands, and the bigger, more attractive fruit from east of the mountains gained preference in the markets. As transporting by boat to market became more expensive, the commercial fruit industry died, and the box factories, saloons, hotels, and rooming houses that went along with it disappeared too. TODAY, REMNANTS OF ORCHARDS are scattered throughout the San Juans, the old gnarled trees bravely blooming and still producing fruit, showering us with countless varieties of *true* heirloom apples and pears.

Wild Blackberry Crema

The English have called this Swedish cream. The Italians call it *panna cotta*. Some call it French cream. In South America, it's called *crema*. Whatever the guise, it is usually a mixture of heavy cream, sour cream, cream cheese, mascarpone, and even yogurt, sweetened and flavored. This version has evolved over the years. For a while, I even put eggs in it. After all the fiddling around, this is my favorite version. I always serve it with a cookie, usually shortbread (see page 26).

For the Crema

> *1½ cups heavy cream*
> *¾ cup sugar*
> *1 vanilla bean, split*
> *1 tablespoon gelatin*
> *¾ cup yogurt*
> *¾ cup sour cream*
> *¼ cup Grand Marnier*

IN A MEDIUM SAUCEPAN OVER MEDIUM HEAT, heat the cream, sugar, seeds from the split vanilla bean, and gelatin to scalding, whisking continuously. Remove from the heat and let cool for a few minutes. Whisk in the yogurt, sour cream, and Grand Marnier. Chill in a mold or individual ramekins.

For the Blackberries

> *3 pints wild blackberries*
> *½ to 1 cup sugar*
> *1 tablespoon limocello or other lemon liqueur*

PURÉE 1 PINT OF THE BLACKBERRIES with sugar to taste and the liqueur. Press the berry sauce through a fine-mesh sieve to remove the seeds. Reserve the remaining whole blackberries for serving.

To Serve

UNMOLD THE CREMA ONTO A PLATTER or plate. Surround with the whole blackberries and some of the sauce.

Serves 6

Chef's Tip: Vanilla beans are expensive. I never throw the empty pod away. Sometimes it goes in the brown sugar, sometimes in the white. Lately, I have been putting the pods in a bottle of brandy; you also could just as easily stick them in a bottle of vodka, Kahlúa, or even pear brandy. Over time, the vanilla flavor will gently infuse whatever you've left it in.

Gooseberry Fool, Coconut Tuiles

Years before I ever considered cooking professionally, my brother gave me a book, the *Larousse Treasury of Country Cooking*. It turned out to be a gem, culling from all the world's cuisines the best and most well-known dishes from each country. A fool, it turns out, is not just that idiot in front of us who fails to signal when making a turn; it is also a classic English dessert. Composed of cooked fresh fruit and sweetened whipped cream, a fool is one of those great simple desserts that works only with the very best ripe fruit and the richest, heaviest cream. The wow factor comes from the juxtaposition of ripe, relatively unsweetened fruit and sweetened whipped cream. The gooseberry is just the kind of fruit for this contrast. On their own, gooseberries are hardly worth the trouble. Dangerous to pick, they have big thorns that will jab right through your gloves. But when the tart berries are cooked with a little sugar, they give up a musky, almost melonlike flavor that couples oh so well with the cream.

For the Fool

2 pints gooseberries
2 to 4 cups sugar, depending on the tartness of the berries
Grated zest of 1 lemon
Grated zest of ½ orange
1 cup water
2 cups heavy cream
2 tablespoons powdered sugar
1 teaspoon rose water

PLACE THE GOOSEBERRIES IN A SAUCEPAN and add the sugar and lemon and orange zests. Add the water, bring to a boil, lower the heat, and simmer for 5 minutes or so, until the berries are tender. Purée the berry mixture through a food mill to remove the seeds, skins, and stems. Chill for at least 1 hour.

IN A LARGE BOWL, using an electric mixer, lightly whip the cream with the powdered sugar and rose water until it barely holds a peak. Fold in the berry purée until the cream is streaked with the fruit. Serve the fool in clear, stemmed glasses with coconut tuiles (recipe follows).

Serves 4 to 6

For the Coconut Tuiles

¼ cup (½ stick) unsalted butter
½ cup sugar
2 egg whites
¼ teaspoon vanilla extract
1 teaspoon unbleached white flour
½ cup shredded, sweetened coconut

PREHEAT THE OVEN TO 350°F. In a medium bowl, using an electric mixer, cream together the butter and sugar. Add the egg whites and vanilla, mix a few seconds, and fold in the flour and coconut.

BUTTER AND FLOUR A LARGE SHEET PAN. Using a lid, coffee cup, or small plate as a pattern, run a knife around the outside edge to make 4-inch circles in the flour. Leave at least 1½ inches between the circles.

PLACE A HEAPING TABLESPOON OF BATTER in the center of each circle. Use the back of a spoon to work the batter to the outer edge of the circle; the batter should be extremely thin but fairly even. Chill for 5 minutes or so before baking.

BAKE FOR 10 TO 12 MINUTES, or until the edges turn golden and the cookies are set. Remove from the oven and immediately roll the cookies into cigarettes, or drape them over a rolling pin, or twist and fold them into a curve. The cookies will crisp up and harden very rapidly. If necessary, reheat the cookies in the oven for a few seconds to make them pliable again.

Makes 18 cookies

Lavender Ice Cream, Hungarian Butterhorns

The summer of 1979 was the summer of the infusion. That spring, my culinary discovery was all about putting flavor into liquid. It started with something as simple as mint tea (mash a big handful of fresh mint leaves in a teapot, cover with boiling water, let sit for ten minutes, infuse!) and ended up with smoky black demi-glaces, aromatic with juniper berries and peppercorns. Moving the flavor of one thing into the flavor of another, creating a third and new flavor from that combination, is what a lot of cuisine is about.

Lavender ice cream is just such an infusion. If you don't have lavender from your garden, most herb and spice purveyors will have some dried lavender. You can dry your own by cutting the flowering spikes in full bloom and hanging a bunch upside down in a cool, dry place. The hanging lets all the flavor and nutrients settle in the flowers.

> *¾ cup honey*
> *2 cups heavy cream*
> *¼ cup dried lavender flowers*
> *6 egg yolks*
> *4 cups half-and-half*
> *¾ cup sugar*
> *Hungarian Butterhorns (see page 24)*

IN A MEDIUM SAUCEPAN, combine the honey, 1 cup of the cream, and the lavender flowers and simmer gently for 20 minutes. Strain the mixture through a fine-mesh sieve and then return it to the saucepan; bring it once again to a gentle simmer.

IN A LARGE BOWL, WHISK THE EGG YOLKS for 3 minutes or so, until they are foamy and well blended. Pour the scalding cream mixture into the egg yolks, whisking continuously. Return the mixture to the saucepan, beat in the remaining cup of cream, and cook for 3 minutes over medium heat, or until the mixture thickens, whisking constantly. Remove from the heat, add the half-and-half and sugar, and whisk to blend. Chill overnight.

FREEZE IN AN ICE CREAM MAKER according to the manufacturer's directions. Serve with Hungarian Butterhorns.

Makes 1½ quarts

Chocolate Blackout Torte

Every self-respecting restaurant must have the over-the-top chocoholic dessert. For more than fifteen years, this was it at Christina's. I estimate I have made this torte more than fifteen hundred times. I have never made it without being vitally interested in the outcome. When I slip the pan into the *bain-marie* and open the oven door, I always have a sense of satisfaction, long before the torte ever makes it to the table.

This torte hardly bakes; it's more like it *sets*. It's also tricky to remove from the pan. If it's cold, it won't come out at all. If it's too warm, it falls apart. My preferred method is to chill it, then slip it in a hot oven for 1 minute, until the outer edge of the torte softens, then briskly upend it on a platter.

Because this torte is so rich, small slivers are plenty.

> *14 ounces Callebaut or other bittersweet chocolate*
> *½ cup espresso*
> *½ cup Kahlúa, Grand Marnier, or Chambord*
> *8 eggs*
> *½ cup sugar*
> *½ cup heavy cream, lightly whipped*
> *2 teaspoons good vanilla extract*

PREHEAT THE OVEN TO 325°F. Butter and flour a 10-inch cake pan. Roughly chop the chocolate and place it in a large bowl. Melt the chocolate with the espresso and liqueur over hot water, or use a double boiler.

IN A LARGE BOWL, whisk together the eggs and sugar until combined. In a small bowl, add the heavy cream and vanilla extract, whip lightly, and set aside. After the chocolate is melted, put the egg mixture over the simmering water and whisk until it is hot to the touch. While hot,

use the whisk attachment to beat the egg mixture until the volume of the eggs triples, about 8 minutes.

POUR 1 CUP of the beaten eggs into the chocolate to lighten the mixture. Fold the chocolate into the remaining eggs with a rubber spatula, taking care not to deflate the eggs. The idea of folding is to incorporate ingredients without removing the air you have previously added. When the mixture is almost blended, add the whipped cream and finish combining.

POUR THE BATTER into the prepared cake pan. Bake in a *bain-marie* (see page 57) until set, about 1 hour. Turn the heat off and let the torte settle in the oven for 1 hour. Chill for 4 hours or overnight.

Note: The torte will keep, refrigerated, for 4 days.

UNMOLD THE TORTE by warming the pan in a hot oven for 1 minute and inverting it onto a platter. Serve with whipped cream (recipe follows).

Serves 10 to 12

For the Whipped Cream

> *1 cup heavy cream*
> *1 teaspoon vanilla extract*
> *1 tablespoon powdered sugar*

PLACE THE CREAM, VANILLA, AND POWDERED sugar in the mixing bowl of an electric mixer. Using the whisk attachment, whip at high speed until the cream doubles in bulk and soft peaks form. Use immediately.

Makes 2 cups

Chocolate Pavé

Recent investigations have shown chocolate to be a healthy snack. Hallelujah! Hailed as an aphrodisiac, a painkiller, and a tranquilizer, chocolate has become as effective as wine for getting a glow on. This chef has a dark secret: I seldom touch the stuff. After working with chocolate for years, I've lost my taste for it. I remember when I loved it, and how satisfying that creamy dark richness was. I just don't have the appetite for it anymore.

Pavé means "paving stone" in French. This might help you to see my pavé for what it is, a brick of chocolate. It is tempered with buttercream and raspberries, but nonetheless it is a slab of chocolate dessert, perfect for a dinner party or buffet. Good-quality chocolate is important in all the chocolate desserts that actually feature chocolate. Bittersweet is sharper to the tongue than semisweet, and real chocolate connoisseurs prefer it. Milk chocolate is for beginners. There are all kinds of chocolate cults, fanatics, and snobs. I stick with my favorites, Callebaut and Valrhona, because I know them so well.

> 14 ounces bittersweet chocolate, such as Callebaut, broken into
> 1-inch pieces
> 2 tablespoons espresso or strong coffee
> ½ cup heavy cream
> ¾ cup (1½ sticks) unsalted butter, at room temperature
> ¼ cup Frangelico
> 1½ cups Raspberry Sauce (see page 29)

MELT THE CHOCOLATE WITH THE ESPRESSO and cream in a double boiler. While the chocolate is melting, line a 1-quart (8½- by 4½-inch) loaf pan with plastic wrap, leaving plenty of extra wrap to drape over the sides. When the chocolate is thoroughly melted, remove it from the heat and whisk in the softened butter and the Frangelico. Pour the chocolate mixture into the loaf pan and finish by smoothing the top of the loaf. Tap the pan on the counter a few times to settle the contents. Fold the extra plastic wrap carefully over the top of the loaf. Chill for at least 6 hours or overnight.

TO SERVE, remove the chilled pavé from the refrigerator and let it sit at room temperature for 5 minutes. Gently lift the edge of the plastic wrap to remove the pavé from the pan. Unwrap it, and cut it into thick slices with a warm knife. Serve at room temperature with raspberry sauce ladled around it.

Serves 10 to 12

Poached Cherries

Cherries are my favorite fruit. Plump, red, and fleshy when ripe, they are elegant and earthy at the same time. Few restaurants bother with cherries anymore. They are problematic because of the pits. It takes time to remove them, but oh boy, is it worth it! The cherries absorb a little of the flavors of the liquid they are poached in (infusion!). Stephen McCarty, at Clear Creek Distillery in Portland, Oregon, did a wonderful thing. He started making distilled spirits along the lines of French *eaux de vie* with fruit from his family's orchards. In the fifteen years since then, his line has expanded to include peaty, dark scotches and other world-class brandies besides the line of raspberry, apple, and pear. Clear Creek's fruit "brandies" are complex and full of fruit character.

5 cups sugar
2 cups water
1 cup red wine vinegar
10 peppercorns
1 cinnamon stick, broken
4 whole cloves
Zest of 1 lemon
2 pounds cherries, pitted
½ cup pear brandy

IN A LARGE POT, place the sugar, water, vinegar, peppercorns, cinnamon stick, cloves, and lemon zest. Bring to a boil, then let simmer, covered, for 20 minutes. Add the cherries and cook for 2 minutes. Remove from the heat and add the brandy. Let the cherries cool in the liquid, then refrigerate. Serve cold.

Serves 6 to 8

Chef's Tip: The minimalist in me likes to serve these cherries very cold in clear, elegant glass. With just some mint fresh from the garden. However, they are perfect over ice cream. For the classic flaming "cherries jubilee" add a tablespoon of 151 rum to the cherry juice in each bowl of ice cream and ignite with a long-handled lighter. This is best when served in a darkened room. Beware: Do not lean over the bowls when you torch them.

Doug Fir Granita

I was groping around for some icy intermezzo to serve at the James Beard House in New York when I came up with this. My standard winter ice was apple-rosemary, because I had lots of cider, and because the rosemary lived all winter. When my February date in New York got close, I realized I was out of both. After checking with my mother, the horticultural expert, to make sure it wasn't poisonous, I made an infusion with Douglas fir boughs and water. When I tasted it, it was like a walk in the winter woods.

The fir boughs must come off the tree in the winter when the weather is cool so that there isn't too much pitch. Boiling water releases the traces of woodsy flavor. The sweet of the sugar and the tart of the vinegar bolster and balance the fir flavor. Freezing deadens flavor on the tongue, so anything meant to be eaten frozen must have a good jolt of boldness to come through the ice. You don't need an ice cream maker for this; you can freeze it in a shallow, nonreactive pan. Stir it a few times while it is freezing; then, when frozen, scrape it into a smaller container.

> 6 cups water
> 1 pound smallish fir fronds on stems
> 2 cups honey
> 2 cups sugar
> ¾ cup apple cider vinegar
> 8 whole peppercorns

COMBINE ALL THE INGREDIENTS IN A LARGE POT and cook, covered, over low heat for 1 hour. Remove from the heat and let cool. Strain in a fine-mesh sieve and discard the solids. Freeze in a shallow, nonreactive pan, stirring occasionally to break up the ice. Serve in chilled clear glasses or bowls.

Makes 1½ quarts

Three Ices: Currant, Blood Orange Maple, and Chocolate

On a hot summer evening nothing cools and refreshes like a fruit ice. The cold of the ice also chills taste buds, and that is why an ice must be intensely flavored to give us the rush of fruit that is so invigorating. I think of the use of sour and sweet in these recipes as rebalancing the fruit. Chocolate, of course speaks for itself

Currant Ice

4 pints fresh currants, puréed and strained
2 cups water
2 to 2½ cups sugar, depending on the sweetness of the currants
1 tablespoon grated lime zest
Juice of 1 lime

COMBINE ALL THE INGREDIENTS and blend well. Freeze in an ice cream maker according to the manufacturer's instructions.

Makes about 1 quart

Blood Orange Maple Ice

4 cups fresh blood orange juice
1⅓ cups maple syrup
⅓ to ½ cup red wine vinegar
Grated zest of 2 oranges
½ cup water

COMBINE ALL THE INGREDIENTS and blend well. Freeze in an ice cream maker according to the manufacturer's instructions.

Makes about 1 quart

Chocolate Ice

2 cups unsweetened cocoa powder
2 cups sugar
1 tablespoon vanilla extract
2 tablespoons espresso or very strong coffee
4 cups water

HEAT ALL THE INGREDIENTS in a saucepan over medium heat and whisk until the chocolate and sugar have dissolved and been incorporated. Whisk and cook for 1 minute or so, until the mixture is fully combined. Cool in the refrigerator for 1 hour, and then freeze in an ice cream maker according to the manufacturer's instructions.

Makes about 1 quart

Raspberry Trifle Torte

Trifle is a classic English dessert. This one is made special by the copious use of ripe raspberries. You can use almost any kind of cake, even angel food or chocolate. If I make it for a crowd, I use a clear glass bowl—mine is a punch bowl, but any big bowl will do. The layers of cream and raspberry are shockingly beautiful. If you want to make individual servings, you could use wine glasses or a fancier dessert glass and have some fun.

Note: If you make this dessert too far in advance the raspberries will "bleed" into the cream and give both the cake and the cream a stained look.

> *2 cups heavy cream*
> *½ cup powdered sugar*
> *1 teaspoon vanilla extract*
> *1 unfrosted 10-inch white or golden génoise layer cake*
> *2 cups Raspberry Sauce (see page 29)*
> *2 pints fresh raspberries*

WHIP THE CREAM WITH THE POWDERED SUGAR and the vanilla until it holds a stiff peak. Cut or break the pieces of cake into a size that works for your serving method. Assemble the trifle by layering: first a bit of cake, then some raspberry sauce, next some whipped cream, then a few whole raspberries; continue layering until you get to the top of the bowl or glass. Garnish the top with some of the whipped cream and whole berries. The torte can be refrigerated for up to 6 hours before serving.

Serves 8

Bumper crop of apples at Old Orchard Farm, Orcas Island.

Index

About the Author

Chef/restaurant owner Christina Orchid was one of the first in the Northwest to commit to the concept of a regional cuisine. She opened her renowned restaurant on Orcas Island, Washington, in the spring of 1980. Inspired by the life and work of French chef Fernand Point, she determined that using the finest local ingredients each season has to offer would provide her customers with the same kind of memorable and delicious meals she had eaten as a child growing up in the islands and working on the family ranch in eastern Washington. Her restaurant has long been a showcase for the wines and foods of the Pacific Northwest and she has carried the bounty of the region and her skills as a chef to countless food events around the country and abroad. Orchid was a contributing editor to *Pacific Northwest the Beautiful Cookbook* and her restaurant has been featured in countless magazines, newspapers, and television programs. Her cameo appearances in the movies *Free Willy II* and *Lethal Weapon 4* cemented her reputation as a true Northwest original. A perennial champion of the Pacific Northwest, Orchid continues to create, reminding her admirers, "you are only as good as the last plate that goes out of your kitchen."